HOW NOW,
BROWN COW?

Other titles include

CLARK, R. and J. McDONOUGH
Imaginery Crimes

FORD, C. and A. SILVERMAN
Cultural Encounters

HAYCRAFT, B. and W. R. LEE
It Depends How You Say It

KNIGHT, M.
Keep in Touch

LAMB, M.
Factions and Fictions

MUGGLESTONE, P. et al
English in Sight 1 & 2 video materials

MUMFORD, S.
In the Mood
Conversation Pieces

ROBERTS, J.
Steps to Fluency

HOW NOW, BROWN COW?

A course in the pronunciation of English, with exercises and dialogues

by

Mimi Ponsonby

Illustrated by

Duncan

ENGLISH LANGUAGE TEACHING

Prentice-Hall International

Englewood Cliffs, N.J. London Mexico New Delhi
Rio de Janeiro Singapore Sydney Tokyo Toronto

First published 1982 by Pergamon Press Ltd.
This edition first published 1987 by
Prentice Hall International (UK) Ltd,
66 Wood Lane End, Hemel Hempstead,
Hertfordshire, HP2 4RG
A division of
Simon & Schuster International Group

Printed and bound in Great Britain at
the University Press, Cambridge

British Library Cataloguing in Publication Data

Ponsonby, Mimi
How now, brown cow?—(English language courses)
1. English language—Textbooks for foreigners
2. English language—Pronunciation
I. Title II. Series
428.1 PE1128

ISBN 0-13-424326-9

3 4 5 92 91 90 89 88

Contents

Introduction

THIS book was originally intended for people studying on their own—businessmen, scientists, would-be teachers—who have learnt their English from the printed page and then find on business trips or international conferences, or even just social occasions, that it is almost impossible to follow a lecture or conversation, and that nobody at all understands *them*; or students wanting to supplement their academic studies with something a little closer to active communication.

However, *How Now, Brown Cow?* is just as suitable for use in a classroom, especially if you have access to a language laboratory. It's *not* necessary to know a lot of English before you begin, though it helps to know a little. The trouble with many people is that they get into bad habits, very often pronouncing English words like sounds of their mother tongue, and the more fluently they speak, using all these incorrect sounds, the more difficult it is to get rid of them. So in a way, it will be easier for you if you *don't* know too much!

Why Pronunciation is necessary

Language is a means of communication. It has three components:

(a) Structures (the patterns that can be seen in these are usually called the *grammar* of the language).

(b) Words that convey meaning (*vocabulary* or *lexis*).

(c) Sound, stress, and intonation patterns, which combine to make up '*Pronunciation*'.

If you communicate *only* through the written word, you will need only the first two of these components. If, on the other hand, you want to be able to understand the *spoken* language, and to be understood, you'll need all three components. Some people think that as long as you know the *words*, and perhaps a smattering of grammar, the *way* you say things doesn't really matter. Well, that's all right as long as all you want the language for is to point to something and say 'How much?', in which case there's not much purpose in your following this course. A child can get what it wants by pointing and saying 'Da! Da!', or screaming till it gets it. But a child soon learns that there are better ways of conveying its needs, and later, that the world and human thought and emotions are far too complex to be expressed merely by pointing or screaming.

Ideally, all three components of language should go hand in hand from the very beginning. If the unfamiliar sounds and pronunciation patterns are mastered early they become so natural that it seems *un*natural to say them incorrectly. All that's left to learn is where the stress lies and how some of the more unusual words are said.

Communication is a two-way process—

1. Understanding other people when they speak.
2. Conveying what you want to say so that other people can understand you.

For the first, understanding, we need—

(a) Knowledge *and*
(b) Awareness, sensitivity.

For the second, conveying meaning, we need—

(a) Knowledge
(b) Awareness *and*
(c) Control.

If you have no idea, for instance, that there's an important difference in English between 's' and 'sh' (phonetically written [s] and [ʃ]), and furthermore you can't distinguish between the two, you won't know how to react if someone asks you to 'bring in the seat'—or was it *sheet*? This situation doesn't seem very serious, but it could be. There are hundreds of stories told of misunderstandings caused by mispronunciation. Sometimes there is laughter, sometimes people walk out in anger, and on at least one occasion there was very nearly an International Incident.

There may be only one, tiny difference between the word the speaker said and the word he *thought* he was saying. Suppose there were two or three 'mistakes' in your pronunciation? The consequences could be

(a) offence to the listener,
(b) misunderstanding by the listener,
(c) complete lack of comprehension by the listener,
(d) a listener so exhausted by the effort of trying to interpret what it is you're trying to say that he gives up and goes and talks to someone else.

Not a very happy prospect! *How Now, Brown Cow?* is designed to minimise the dangers.

How to use this book

The book is divided into fifty-eight units, each of which deals with either a single phoneme or a characteristic feature of British English pronunciation. Each unit begins with an explanation of how to produce a particular sound or handle a particular feature. This is followed by exercises, either for repetition and practice or for recognition and distinction of sounds. There are also exercises on syllable stress.

With exercises for *repetition and practice* it is always best to *listen first without looking at the text*. The written word can so often interfere with one's perception of an unfamiliar sound. As you repeat, check constantly to make sure that you're carrying out carefully the instructions at the top of the page, and that your speech organs are all in the correct position. Listen very attentively to the sounds on the tape, and imitate these as exactly as you can, parrotwise, without, for the time being, worrying about meaning. Think initially *only* of sound. This requires discipline but is worth the effort. If you have a second tape recorder on which you can record your own voice, this is the best way to listen to yourself dispassionately, as if the voice belonged to someone else.

Remember, acquiring a complex skill like a language requires both awareness and control, and these can only be achieved through constant practice. To make this practice more varied, there are words in groups, as well as tongue-twisters, nursery rhymes and proverbs. Under the heading of 'Proverbs' I have included common idioms and an occasional quotation.

Once you feel that you've mastered the *sound*, look at the words as they're written. You'll be surprised at the spelling—but remember the *sound* remains constant. Keep checking your pronunciation as you repeat the sounds, either in unison with or after the tape. Be aware all the time of your speech organs—the shape of your mouth, the position of your tongue, voicing or lack of it, and so on. Experiment with sounds. Practise combinations that make no sense, simply to exercise your muscles —'Waa wee waa wee' or 'Hoe go hoe go'—that sort of thing. Never be afraid to exaggerate—you can always tone it down.

The exercises for *discrimination* are designed to encourage you to listen accurately and to refine your awareness of the differences between sounds which to the untrained ear appear indistinguishable. There is no reason why these exercises shouldn't be used for practice, too.

The same applies to the exercises on *syllable stress*. Use them first of all to sharpen your sensitivity to stress within words and later to rhythm in longer speech, and carry this sensitivity into real life so that you're also aware of these things in real conversation. Then practise them yourself, making the stressed syllables louder, longer and higher than the rest. Again, don't be afraid to exaggerate.

At the bottom of each left-hand page, printed upside down, are the answers to questions in which you have to make decisions. Do try not to look before you've made up your own mind what the answer should be. Even if you're wrong, you will have learnt something. And you can go back and listen again and try to discover *why* you were wrong.

Finally, we come to the *dialogues*, which all these exercises have been leading up to. Now we practise the particular sound or feature of pronunciation with which the unit is concerned. The situations are, perhaps, a little fantastic but the language is ordinary—at least, as ordinary as is possible if one's concentrating on one particular sound.

Each dialogue has been recorded like this:

1. The complete conversation with both parts read by native speakers.
2. The conversation repeated, but the second voice omitted.
3. The conversation repeated once more, with the first voice omitted.

Only enough time has been left on the tape for you to say the speech at the same speed as the original native speaker. If this is not long enough for you at first, switch off the machine each time it is your turn, but try to increase your speed and fluency so that eventually the conversation flows and you answer the first speaker and he or she answers you as naturally as if the other person was in the room with you. Practise if you possibly can until you feel you have made some improvement. But do not work any one dialogue or speech to death. You can always return to a unit after you have worked on others. In fact, since, like driving a car or flying an aeroplane, speech demands controlling a number of diverse skills *at the same time* (it is not much use saying 'I'm changing gear—how can I be expected to steer?'), and since each dialogue must obviously contain a great many features of speech other than the one it's primarily intended to practise, *all* the dialogues are useful for practising *all* aspects of pronunciation.

What you need to know before you begin

I have tried, as far as possible, to keep the explanations of so-called 'rules' simple and untechnical. But there are one or two basic and *very* important concepts that appear again and again throughout the book and which it would be sensible to explain once and for all now so that instead of repeating the explanation I can simply use the word or phrase that refers to it—this, after all, is the purpose of all specialised terminology.

The terms I want to explain are:

1. '*Phoneme*'

A phoneme is the smallest unit of sound that *makes a difference to meaning* in any given language. The sounds of your 'target language' (the language you are trying to learn—in this case British English) may either (a) not exist or (b) exist but be replaceable without altering meaning by another, fairly close sound. In some languages [w] and [v] are interchangeable, both probably being pronounced somewhere between the two sounds as said in English. Or [l] and [r] may not be phonemic. In Finnish and Estonian the lengths of vowels and consonants alter the meaning of otherwise similar words, but to an English person the difference between the lengths is at first both impossible to hear and impossible to reproduce. Each language has its own particular phonemic system. If you are going to be able to understand and make people understand you in English, it is obvious that you must (a) recognise the English phonemes and (b) pronounce them correctly yourself.

2. *The terms 'voiced' and 'voiceless'*

When you pronounce a sound, you can either vibrate your vocal cords (producing a 'voiced' sound) or push the air straight up from your lungs and out of your mouth (a 'voiceless' sound).

Many English *consonant sounds* can be grouped into pairs, both sounds of which are produced in exactly the same way except that one is voiced and the other is voiceless; [b] and [p], [v] and [f] are examples. Each sound in these pairs is phonemic, so it is very important to make the difference between them—this one feature of voicedness or voicelessness—very clear, and also to be aware of it when you are listening.

There are several ways to check whether you are pronouncing these sounds correctly. First, put your fingers on your Adam's apple and say [v], which is a voiced sound, and a good one to practise with because you can hold on to it. You should feel a strong vibration. If you say the voiceless equivalent, [f], you should feel no vibration at all. Better still, cover your ears with your hands and make the two sounds.

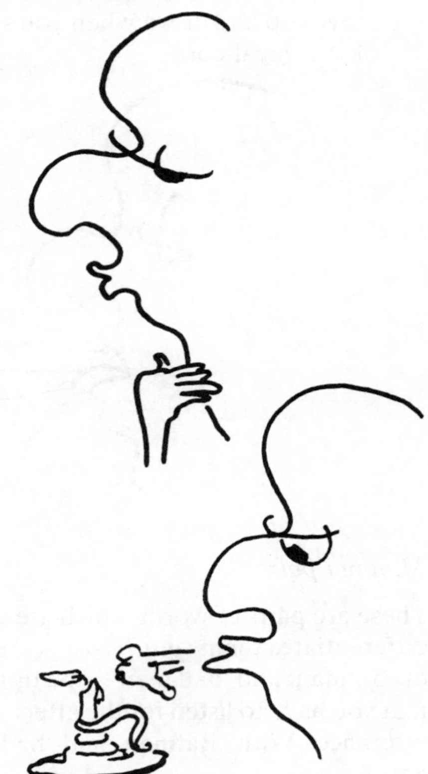

With voiceless sounds, the air that you expel should come out at such a force that it blows a candle out or a feather off your hand. At least you should be able to feel the air if you hold your hand in front of your mouth. With the voiced sounds, there should be no more than a tiny explosion of air. All *vowels* are voiced.

3. *The speech organs*

These are all the parts of the head that you use to make sounds. They are:

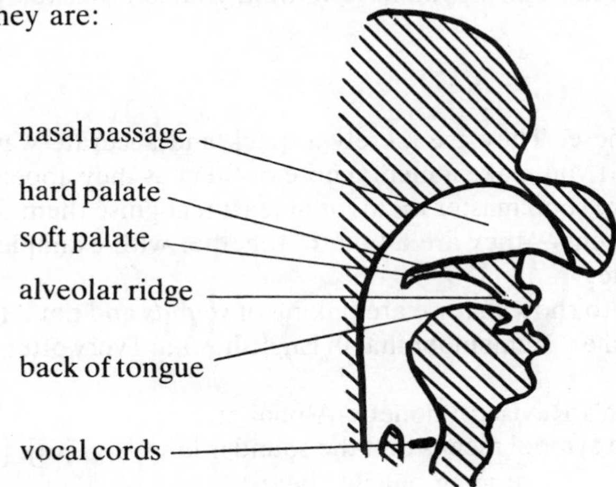

Teeth—top (or upper) and bottom (or lower).
Tongue—tip, middle, back.
Alveolar ridge—the ridge of bone just behind the top teeth.
Vocal cords—two parallel muscles like strings of a harp, which vibrate to produce 'voiced' sounds.

Adam's apple—the bump in the front of your throat which moves up and down when you swallow. This is just in front of the vocal cords.

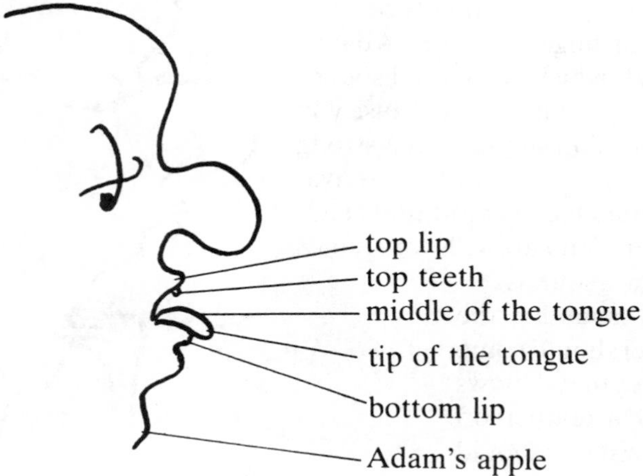

4. *Minimal pairs*

These are pairs of words which are *almost* exactly the same. Only one small thing differentiates them (*pin:bin* or *pin:pan*, for instance). Sometimes—as in the case of 'Batman' and 'bad man'—the difference between the pronunciation is so slight that you have to listen for the effect the change of consonants has on the rest of the utterance. With 'Batman' and 'bad man' it's the difference in the length of the vowel.

Because these tiny differences may not exist in your language, or may not be important, but *are* phonemic in English, you have to train yourself to listen very carefully.

Phonetic symbols

Do not, please, be afraid of these. They are merely a quick and accurate way of referring to particular sounds. If you make a mental note of them as they appear at the top of each unit you will very soon master them, or at least recognise them. If in doubt, look at the table of contents—they are all there, together with examples in ordinary script to act as a guide.

They are in square brackets [ ] to show that we are talking of *sounds* and not letters of the alphabet or units of grammar. Remember that in English, sound very often has no relation to spelling!

The system followed is Gimson's Revised Phonetic Alphabet.

Note that a mark (ː) following a symbol means that the sound is long, e.g. [ɑː], [ɜː].

iː as in b**ea**t, b**ea**d	ɔː as in b**ough**t, b**oa**rd
ɪ as in b**i**t, b**i**d	ʊ as in f**oo**t, g**oo**d
e as in b**e**t, b**e**d	uː as in l**oo**se, l**o**se
æ as in b**a**t, b**a**d	ʌ as in c**u**t, c**o**me
ɑː as in b**ar**k, b**ar**n	ɜː as in b**ir**th, g**ir**l
ɒ as in b**o**ss, b**o**mb	ə as in **a**mong, sof**a**

eɪ as in **late**, **laid**
əʊ as in **coat**, **code**
aɪ as in **write**, **ride**
aʊ as in ab**out**, al**ou**d
ɔɪ as in **voice**, **boys**
ɪə as in **pierce**, **beard**
eə as in sc**ar**ce, st**air**s
ʊə as in s**ure** (also pronounced [ʃɔː])

θ as in **th**ink, mon**th**
ð as in **th**en, brea**the**
ʃ as in **sh**ip, wa**sh**
ʒ as in mea**s**ure, rou**ge**
tʃ as in **ch**in, wat**ch**
dʒ as in **j**ump, bri**dge**
ŋ as in si**ng**er, thi**ng**
j as in **y**es, opi**n**ion

Now you're ready to begin. But just before you leave me and set off on your own, may I make one request? If you have problems that I have not dealt with in the book, or if you can find peculiar spelling that I haven't included, or you know other proverbs and funnier tongue-twisters, do let me know. I shall be delighted to receive them. They can always go into the next edition!
And now, off you go. Don't expect it all to be easy. And don't worry if occasionally you feel you'll *never* get it right. All learning is hard work. But at the same time it should always be fun!

To MCW,

who pointed my nose in the right direction

HOW NOW, BROWN COW?

1. [p] pin

The first six sounds we are going to examine are called 'plosives' because you build up a pressure of air and release it like a small explosion. To produce the first one, [p], press your lips together, let the air from the lungs build up behind them and then blow it out suddenly. You should be able to blow out a candle or a feather off your hand. Let the air come straight up from the lungs, as this is a *voiceless* sound. Keep blowing through the vowel that follows; e.g. 'park', 'pin'. Listen carefully to exercise A on the tape before you try. The speaker is exaggerating, but only a little. When you practise, exaggerate too.
Sometimes it helps to think there is an 'h' after the 'p'. As if you were saying 'p-hin' (often written [pʰɪn]).

PRACTICE

A. *Hold your hand upright in front of your mouth, so that your fingers are just touching your nose. Make sure that you feel a definite explosion of air each time you say [p].*

(a)

Percy	pass	pet	presume	expensive	
perfect	put	poor	practical	expect	
purpose	pot	post	pride	explain	
people	pay	pack	pretty	explore	
Popplewell	pound	pun	present	explode	
			silent 'p'		
porridge	puce	uphill	(p)neumonia	cu(p)board	cou(p)
possible	puny	upheaval	(p)salm	ras(p)berry	cor(ps)
parcel	computer	upholstery	(p)sychology	recei(p)t	

(b) Practice makes perfect.
The proof of the pudding is in the eating.
Promises and piecrusts are made to be broken.
Penny plain, twopence coloured.
To rob Peter to pay Paul.
Peter Piper picked a peck of pickled pepper. If Peter Piper picked a peck of pickled pepper, where's the peck of pickled pepper Peter Piper picked?

B. *Listen to the tape. Which is s/he saying? Underline the right word in each pair.*

(a) pig/big
(b) pill/fill
(c) pen/ten
(d) pick/thick
(e) pat/bat
(f) post/boast
(g) pan/can
(h) pole/hole
(i) pop/bop

Answers: B. (a) pig (b) pill (c) ten (d) thick (e) bat (f) post (g) can (h) pole (i) bop

DIALOGUE 1. A present for Penelope

PETER: Pass the pepper, will you, please, Percy, old chap?
PERCY: Pepper? You're not proposing to put pepper on your porridge?
PETER: Shut up, Percy! Why do you always presume that I'm stupid?
PERCY: Well, stop snapping and explain the purpose of the pepper pot.
PETER: It's perfectly simple. I want to compare our pepper pot with the pepper pot I've bought as a present for Penelope Popplewell.
PERCY: A practical—but pretty expensive—present!
PETER: Well, she's a super person. I thought perhaps, if you happened to be passing the Post Office . . . Could you possibly pop the parcel in the post?
PERCY: Am I expected to pay the postage on this pepper pot for Penelope Popplewell?
PETER: Percy, you're impossible! I may be poor but I have my pride! Here's £1 for the postage.

2. [b] bin

Your mouth is in the same position as for [p], but this time the sound is *voiced*, that is, the vocal cords behind your Adam's apple are vibrated. Put your fingers on your throat or over your ears each time, to check that you really are making a difference between the voiced and voiceless sounds. Don't be afraid to exaggerate. Make sure there is only the smallest explosion of air.

PRACTICE

A.

						silent 'b'	
(a)	bit	baby	blanket	brother	trouble	clim(b)	de(b)t
	bat	balcony	blades	brandy	table	com(b)	dou(b)t
	but	bottle	bless you	breathe	problem	thum(b)	su(b)tle

(b) *Now practise lengthening the vowel before the [b] like this:*
tap (very short) : ta-a-ab (as long as you like).

tap/tab	lope/lobe	harp/harbour	simple/symbol
sheep/Sheba	Caple/cable	baps/Babs	tripe/tribe

(c) His bark's worse than his bite.
The blind leading the blind.
Your eyes are bigger than your belly.
A bird in the hand is worth two in the bush.

Beauty will buy no beef.
Blind as a bat.
Bold as brass.

B. *Which is the speaker saying? Remember, when there's a voiced consonant sound at the end of a syllable, the vowel before it is lengthened. If the consonant sound is voiceless, the vowel is short.*

(a) What a beautiful golden peach!/beach!

(b) The pills/bills are on the table.

(c) The mop/mob fell on him.

(d) He threw off the rope/robe and ran away.

C. *Mixed voiced/voiceless. Say slowly, then faster and faster, but always thinking carefully whether you are saying [p] or [b].*

(a) The butcher put the pork spareribs into a brown paper bag.
(b) Betty's prepared beautiful puff pastry for the blackberry and apple pie.
(c) Peter's big pink pig's broken the tips of Bill's best rhubarb plants.

Answers: B. (a) beach (b) pills (c) mop (d) robe

DIALOGUE 2. Brandy in the baby's bottle!

Telephone rings. Brr . . . brr brr.

BOB: Bob Batterby.

BABS: Oh Bob, this is Babs. I'm baby-sitting for Betty and my brother Bill. I'm sorry to bother you but . . .

BOB: What's the trouble? No problem's too big when Bob's on the job!

BABS: Oh stop being stupid, Bob. It's baby. I put her on the balcony on a blanket with a biscuit to bite on and I think a bit of biscuit . . . She can't breathe.

BOB: Bang her on the back, between the shoulder blades.

BABS: I've banged her till she's black and blue.

BOB: Try putting a bit of brandy in her bottle.

BABS: Brandy in the baby's bottle! Oh *Bob*!

BOB: Sorry, Babs. Sounds bad. I'd better bicycle over. Be with you before you can say 'bread and butter'.

BABS: Bless you, Bob. 'Bye 'bye. Be quick!

3. [t] tie

Press the tip of your tongue against the ridge of bone behind and above your top teeth (the alveolar ridge) so that no air can get through. Build up the pressure of air behind this barrier, and then break the pressure by opening your mouth a little and removing your tongue from the ridge so that the air rushes out. Carry on the rush of air through the vowel sound that follows, as you did with [p], so that the word 'tin' sounds like 't-hin' or even 'tsin'. Exaggerate this aspiration to begin with as you practise.

PRACTICE

A.

(a)

time	torn	twelve	trousers	what	after	Templetons
tell	taxi	twenty	tried	late	water	tempted
town	telephone	between	transport	night	empty	extravagant

(b) *Past forms with '-ed' following a voiceless consonant sound (except [t]—see page 8).*

hoped	looked	puffed	missed	wished	fetched	mixed
hopped	asked	laughed	passed	crashed	watched	boxed

(c) *'th' pronounced [t].*
Anthony, Thomas and Theresa Thompson live at No. 10 Chatham Street, Walton-on-Thames, next to Thyme Cottage.

(d) *Silent 't'.*

chris(t)en	cas(t)le	ches(t)nut	sof(t)en	cabare(t)
lis(t)en	wres(t)le	Chris(t)mas	of(t)en	balle(t)
glis(t)en	whis(t)le	exac(t)ly	mus(t)n't	croque(t)

(e) Better late than dead on time.
A storm in a teacup.
To fall between two stools.
On the tip of your tongue.
If at first you don't succeed, try, try and try again.
Temptations are like tramps—let one in and he returns with his friends.

B. *Listen to the tape and fill in the missing words. Then say the sentences aloud.*

(a) These . . . . are . . . . Why . . . . you . . . them?
(b) . . . . answer the . . . . I . . . . you . . . .
(c) The . . . . arrive . . . . a . . . . , so you'd . . . . a . . . . the . . . .
(d) . . was . . a . . . . . . or . . . . the . . . . was . . . . .

Answers: B. (a) These trousers are too tight. Why don't you try them?
(b) Don't answer the telephone until I tell you to.
(c) The train won't arrive till a quarter to eight, so you'd better take a taxi straight to the concert.
(d) It was at a minute or two to two that the teacher was shot.

DIALOGUE 3. Waiting for Templetons

TESSA: What time did you tell Templetons to get here, Martin?
MARTIN: Any time between 10 and 12.
TESSA: But it's after two! They're terribly late!
MARTIN: Why didn't you contact United Transport as I told you?
TESSA: Peter Thompson said that Templetons were better.
MARTIN: Tessa! Peter Thompson's a director of Templetons. Oh! blast it! I've torn my trousers on the radiator!
TESSA: Oh Martin, do take care! . . . Hadn't we better telephone?
MARTIN: I've tried. The telephone's not connected yet.
TESSA: And the water's still cut off. We can't just wait here all afternoon in an empty flat with no water and no telephone.
MARTIN: How uninviting an empty flat is.
TESSA: And it seems tiny, too, now, doesn't it?
MARTIN: I'm tempted to take a taxi straight into town and stay the night in a hotel.
TESSA: How extravagant! But what a delightful thought!

4. [d] die

This is the voiced equivalent of [t], so the tongue starts in the same position, against the alveolar ridge, and the lower jaw is pulled down and the tongue withdrawn from the ridge to release the pressure. However, as this is a voiced sound, there will be no rush of air but only a tiny explosion. Don't forget to check on your vibration, either with your fingers on your Adam's apple, or by covering your ears. And don't forget to lengthen any vowel sound immediately before the [d].

PRACTICE

A.

(a)

		long vowel		*silent 'd'*	
do	dreary	bed	date	han(d)some	gran(d)mother
day	drab	rode	daughter	han(d)kerchief	gran(d)father
dog	drive	afraid	don't	han(d)cuff	We(d)nesday

past tense '-ed'
after voiced consonant

lived	sagged	seized
called	banged	waged

after 't', 'd' [ɪd]

wanted	patted	added	landed
waited	acted	loaded	ended

(b) *Don't forget to lengthen the vowel if it's followed by a voiced consonant.*

tame	mate	time	spite	tram	mat	toll	coat
dame	made	dime	spied	dram	mad	dole	code

(c) All dressed up like a dog's dinner.
Never say die until you're dead.
Between the devil and the deep blue sea.
Dull as ditch water.
Dead as a door nail.

B. *Which is s/he saying?*

(a) I've put a tent/dent in the car.

(b) This seed/seat should be kept in the garden shed.

(c) I saw two men pushing a trunk/drunk into the taxi.

(d) I'm afraid he's a heart/hard case.

(e) I think it's thirsty./Thursday.

C. *One word in each sentence (3 words in (f)) makes the whole sentence into nonsense. Which are the words? And what ought they to be?*

(a)
(b)
(c)
(d)
(e)
(f)

Answers: B. (a) tent (b) seat (c) drunk (d) heart (e) Thursday
(a) I can't turn my tap off. It keeps *tripping* (dripping).
(b) Tell Dora to harden her *hard* (heart) and turn the cat out.
(c) Do stop *dreading* (treading) on my dress, Tony!
(d) I ate the most delicious *drought* (trout) for dinner last night.
(e) The goat kept *budding* (butting) me from behind. It was most irritating.
(f) I *sad* (sat) down on the *seed* (seat) that has just been painted and got my trousers covered in red *strides* (stripes).

DIALOGUE 4. All dressed up for a date with David

DONALD: And what's my darling daughter doing all dressed up?
DEIRDRE: I've got a date with David, Daddy. We're going to a dance at Dudley Head, with Dan and Ada Dodd.
DONALD: David? Not that dreary lad who came to dinner on Friday and trod on the dog? Deirdre, he's dreadful!
DEIRDRE: Oh Daddy! He's *divine*! I adore him!
DONALD: I found him dreadfully dull, I'm afraid. You know, that dress doesn't do anything for you, my dear. Dark red! Darling, it's so deadening, so dreadfully drab!
DEIRDRE: Oh Daddy! Why is everything I do dreadful these days? (*The front door-bell rings.*) Oh, there's David! I must dash.
DONALD: Is he driving? Don't let him drink. And don't forget, you said you'd be in bed by midnight.
DEIRDRE: Oh Daddy!

5. [k] cut

Raise the back of your tongue and press it against your soft palate at the back of your mouth cavity, completely blocking the passage of air. As with [p] and [t], as soon as this blockage is released the air rushes out and the voiceless sound is produced. And as with [p] and [t], there is a great deal of aspiration, so practise saying [k-hæn] (can), [k-hi:p] (keep), [k-hɪt] (kit).

PRACTICE

A.

(a)

				'ch' (mostly from Greek)	
cash	Mike	market	clock	ache	stomach
case	take	taking	neck	school	monarch
come	park	broken	back	chaos	mechanic
coin	keep	baker	duck	Christmas	archaeology
car	kid	crikey	sick	echo	archipelago

[ks]	*[kw]*	*but* *[k]*	*silent 'k' before 'n'*
taxi	quick	quay	(k)now
six	quite	quarter	(k)nock
accent	quiet	conquer	(k)nee
mixed	quality	cheque	(k)nife
success	question	mosquito	(k)new

(b) Curiosity killed the cat.
To cut your coat according to your cloth.
Cool as a cucumber.
The pot calling the kettle black.

A cat may look at a king.
To come a cropper.
Catch as catch can.
To kill a wife with kindness.

B. *Question and answer (this is best done in pairs).*

1. Can you talk in Cockney to a crowd in Connaught Square?
   Of *course* I can talk in Cockney to a crowd in Connaught Square.
2. Can you coat a coffee cake with Cornish clotted cream?
   Of *course* I can . . .
3. Can you quickly kick a crooked Coca-Cola can?
   Of *course* I can . . .
4. Can you catch a cuckoo in a broken wicker cage?
   Of *course* I can . . .

C. *Which of these words are said twice?*

(a) sack/sag
(b) pick/pig
(c) cap/gap
(d) came/game
(e) coat/goat
(f) card/guard
(g) peck/peg
(h) class/glass

Answers: C. (a) sack (b) pig (c) gap (d) came (e) coat (f) guard (g) peg (h) class

DIALOGUE 5. Cash in the ice-cream carton

COLIN: O.K., Mike. At six o'clock you take a taxi to the bank. Max will come out with the cash in a cream-coloured case . . .
MIKE: I'm to collect the cash?
COLIN: Of course. Don't ask questions. Just concentrate.
MIKE: Colin, if they catch me I'll confess.
COLIN: Keep quiet, can't you? At a quarter to six Coco will be parked at the corner of the Market Square.
MIKE: I'll scream. I'm a coward. The kids at school . . .
COLIN: Pack the cash in the ice-cream carton in the back of the car and make your way as quick as you can back to the café.
MIKE: Colin, I'm scared.
COLIN: Oh crikey, Mick! You do make me sick!

6. [g] gut

Like [p]:[b] and [t]:[d], [k] and [g] are a pair, the only difference in the two sounds being that the first is voiceless, the second voiced. So place your tongue in the same position as for [k] but do not let the air rush out, and control the sound from your vocal cords, which should be vibrating. Until you are quite confident that you can make the correct sound every time, always check for this vibration. Remember to lengthen a preceding vowel.

PRACTICE

A.

(a)

					'-gue'
go	Gran	grumble	glass	ago	plague
get	great	Grandfather	glove	again	league
good	grey	grocer	Gladys	begin	prologue
give	angry	telegram	glade	together	dialogue
gold	Greece	disgraceful	igloo	regatta	synagogue

Remember to lengthen the vowel (ba-a-ag)			*silent 'g'*		*[nj]*
bag	bog	target	(g)naw	si(g)n	poignant
flag	fog	organ	(g)nat	campai(g)n	cognac
sag	jog	eager	(g)nome	forei(g)n	

(b) (i) *Say each column downwards, taking care to make the initial sound exaggeratedly voiced or voiceless.*
(ii) *Repeat the words, but reading across the page, so that you have alternate voiced/voiceless sounds. Again, make the difference very clear.*

pin	bin	pan	ban	pay	bay
tin	din	tan	Dan	Tay	day
kin	begin	can	began	Kay	gay

(c) To kill the goose that lays the golden egg.
All that glisters is not gold.
Go and teach your grandmother to suck eggs.
As good as gold.
To give as good as you get.

B. *Which is s/he saying?*

(a) Put this in the back,/bag, will you?

(b) I thought I caught a glimpse of the coast./ghost.

(c) Your class/glass is in there.

(d) I found a cap/gap in the hedge.

(e) You haven't drawn that ankle/angle very well.

Answers: B. (a) back (b) ghost (c) class (d) gap (e) angle

DIALOGUE 6. Eggs from the Greek grocer

GLADYS: Gran, I'm hungry. Can we go home?
GRANNY: Grumbling again, Gladys! A great big girl like you. Now take my grey bag and go and get some eggs from the grocer, there's a good girl.
GLADYS: But Gran . . .
GRANNY: I'm going to send a telegram to your grandfather. Oh, give me my glasses before you go. In the green and gold grosgrain case.
GLADYS: But Granny . . .
GRANNY: Don't giggle, girl, I'm beginning to get angry. Go and get the eggs.
GLADYS: But Gran, it's no good my going to the grocer. He's gone away. He goes back to Greece every August. He's Greek.
GRANNY: Gone to Greece? How disgraceful!

7. Syllable stress

In words of more than one syllable, the syllables do not all have equal stress. There is usually one that has particularly strong stress. This means that on this syllable your voice is louder and usually pitched higher, and you hang on to the syllable considerably longer than on the other syllables of that word. Different stressing can change the meaning of a word or make it completely unrecognisable.

A few general rules

(a) Always stress the syllable *before* one that's pronounced [ʃn] -ssion/-tion, [ʃs] -cious/-tious, [ʃl] -cial/-tial, etc., e.g. atténtion, spácious, artifícial.
(b) In words ending '-ic', '-ical', '-ically', the stress is on the syllable *before* '-ic', *except* Árabic, aríthmetic, lúnatic, héretic, pólitics, rhétoric (*but* adjectives: arithmétic, herétical, polítical, rhetórical).
(c) A great many words are stressed on the last syllable but two, e.g. illúminate, thermómeter, geólogy, philósopher. Words ending in '-ólogy', '-ónomy', '-ósophy', '-ólogist', etc., always follow this rule.
(d) Words ending in '-ese' have the stress on this syllable (Chinése, journalése).
(e) Do not stress the negative prefix attached to an adjective (póssible, impóssible; líterate, illíterate) *except*: nówhere, nóthing, nóbody, nónsense.

PRACTICE

A. *Exaggerate the stressing as much as you can—i.e. make the stressed syllable louder, higher and longer than the unstressed ones.*

(a) completion efficient invasion financial advantageous vivacious
(b) photogenic scientific materialistic geographical musical technical
(c) psychology/psychologist meteorology/meteorologist ideology/ideologist
(d) Chinese Japanese Portuguese Cantonese Balinese Viennese
(e) organised/disorganised complete/incomplete attractive/unattractive legal/illegal where/nowhere sense/nonsense

B. *Practise shifting the stress.*

photograph	politics	competing	analyse
photographer	political	competitor	analysis
photographic	politician	competition	analytical

C. *Listen to the dialogue. Where are the stresses?*

photography	develop	photographic	amateurs	political
institute	photographs	possibility	politician	competitive
career	technical	competition	distinguished	politics

Answers: C. photógraphy / ínstitute / caréer / devélop / phótographs / téchnical / photográphic / possibílity / competítion / ámateurs / politícian / distínguished / polítical / compétitive / pólitics

DIALOGUE 7: Photography or politics?

DIANA: What have you decided to do after college, Jeremy?

JEREMY: I'm going to take up photography. Mr McKenzie's recommended the course at the Institute. He believes I could make a career as a photographer.

DIANA: You'll have to develop your own photographs. That requires technical skill. Jeremy, you're not a technician! And photographic materials are very expensive.

JEREMY: Well, Diana, Mr McKenzie thinks there's a possibility I might win the *Observer* competition. I sent in four entries. All the competitors are amateurs, like myself.

DIANA: I detest competitions. I never agree with the decision of the judges! I'm going to be a politician. I shall become the most distinguished woman on the political scene!

JEREMY: I thought you hated competing! Don't tell me politics isn't competitive!

8. [f] fun

This is an easy sound to make. Bite your bottom lip gently between your teeth. Build up pressure behind this wall of your top teeth and bottom lip, but don't puff out your cheeks, then open your mouth just enough to let air through, and blow, as you did with [p], [t] and [k]. You should be able to blow a feather off your hand. Remember to keep on the aspiration through the vowel that follows.

PRACTICE

A.

						[fj]
(a)	fine	fling	fry	awful	left	few
	fox	fly	freeze	thief	lift	fumes
	fun	flew	frost	off	loft	fuel
	far	float	Freddie	stiff	puffed	future
	forest	fluff	Francis	puff	after	furious

'ph' (mainly from Greek)	*'-gh'*			*silent 'f'*
philosophy	laugh	enough	trough	halfpenny
photograph	draught	rough	cough	[heɪpnɪ]
telephone				
hyphen				
Philip				

(b) *Now some threesomes to say very quickly:*

fat	fox	father	life	lift	gaffer
fit	flocks	feather	leaf	loft	duffer
foot	frocks	further	loaf	left	loofa

(c) Out of the frying pan into the fire.
Fine feathers make fine birds.
Birds of a feather flock together.
Enough is as good as a feast.
Fit as a fiddle.
Laugh and grow fat.
Few and far between.
The fat's in the fire.

B. *Which is s/he saying? Put a circle round the right word.*

(a) life/like (b) foot/put (c) fail/sail (d) loft/lost (e) tough/touch (f) fuel/duel (g) laughs/last (h) fry/try

C. *Listen to the dialogue. Which are the stressed syllables?*

Daphne	afternoon	fiftieth	fabulous
sofa	forest	awful	Felicity
Friday	Fiona	furious	fancy

Answers: B. (a) life (b) put (c) sail (d) loft (e) tough (f) duel (g) laughs (h) try
C. Dáphne, sófa, Fríday, afternóon, fórest, Fióna, fíftieth, áwful, fúrious, fábulous, Felícity, fáncy

DIALGOUE 8. A fine, flashy fox fur

FELICITY: That's a fine, flashy fox fur you've flung on the sofa, Daphne.
DAPHNE: Yes, I found it on Friday afternoon in Iffley Forest.
FELICITY: But, Daphne! That's Fiona's fox fur—her fiftieth birthday gift from Freddie. You are awful! Fiona will be furious.
DAPHNE: Well, if Fiona left her fur in the forest . . .
FELICITY: Fiona leave her fabulous fox fur in the forest? Stuff and nonsense! You're a thief! Take it off!
DAPHNE: Felicity! What a fuss over a faded bit of fluff! Anyway, fancy Fiona in a fur! She's *far* too fat!

9. [v] victory

The position of the mouth is the same as that for [f], but this is a voiced consonant. Remember to try saying it with your hands over your ears, or your fingers on your throat. There must be no vibration with [f] but lots of air; lots of vibrations with [v] but very little air. Some of the air can come out at the sides of your mouth. When you say [v], try to make your lips tingle.

PRACTICE

A. *Exaggerate the vibration and hang on to the [v] as long as you can.*

(a)

Victor	violet	ever	over	approve	five
velvet	vodka	travel	envious	leave	drove
vivid	verse	university	advise	wave	give

N.B. nephews, Stephen—both pronounced [v].

(b) *Now, as fast as you can:*

van	vast	vowel	live	weave
vain	vest	veil	love	wave
vine	voiced	vole	leave	wove

(c) *[f]/[v] contrast.*

fat/vat few/view Fife/five safe/save offer/hover
leaf/leaves calf/calves half/halves thief/thieves off/of

(d) An iron hand in a velvet glove.
Men were deceivers ever.
Vanity of vanities, all is vanity.
Virtue is its own reward.
All's fair in love and war.
If I say it over and over and over again, eventually I'll improve.

B. *Which is s/he saying?*

(a) Is that your new Shaeffer?/shaver?

(b) We'll meet at Fife./five.

(c) We managed to get a few/view of the horses across the valley.

(d) Leave them alone—they're my wife's./wives.

C. *Listen to the dialogue. Which are the stressed syllables?*

Liverpool	marvellous	approve	advise	overdo
invitation	overcoat	professors	anniversary	caviar
university	enough	disapproval	Valentine	believe
creative	reversible	November	invasion	envious

Answers: B. (a) Shaeffer (b) five (c) view (d) wife's
C. Liverpool / invitation / university / creative / marvellous / overcoat / enough / reversible / approve / professors / disapproval / November / advise / anniversary / Valentine / invasion / overdo / caviar / believe / envious

DIALOGUE 9. A visit to Vladivostok

OLIVER: Victor, have you ever visited Vladivostok?

VICTOR: Never. In fact, I haven't travelled further than Liverpool.

OLIVER: I've had an invitation from the University of Vladivostok to give a survey of my own creative verse.

VICTOR: How marvellous!

OLIVER: Will my navy overcoat be heavy enough, I wonder? It's long-sleeved and reversible. And I've got a pair of velvet Levis—rather a vivid violet! Do you think they'll approve?

VICTOR: I should think the professors will view violet Levis with violent disapproval. When do you leave?

OLIVER: On the 7th of November.

VICTOR: I don't advise you to travel on the 7th. It's the anniversary of the Valentine Invasion. And for heaven's sake, Oliver, don't overdo the caviar. Or the vodka.

OLIVER: Victor, I do believe you're envious!

10. [w] will

To make this sound, hold your hand vertically in front of your face, nearly touching your nose. Now kiss your hand. Holding this position (you can take your hand away but keep your mouth pursed, looking as in the diagram on right if you look in the mirror) give a long [uː] sound. Keep making the sound but open your jaw about half-way. This will pull your lips apart and change the quality of the sound. It is this sliding movement that makes up the [w] sound. You should be able to put your finger right into your mouth all the time. Remember we are talking of a *sound*, not necessarily represented by the letter 'w'. Syllables ending in [uː], [əʊ] or [aʊ], and followed by a vowel insert a [w] sound, whether this is written or not (*fluent*, *poetical*, *ploughing*). This is true even if the vowel is at the beginning of the next word (see Linking, p. 44), e.g. *two*[w] *answers*, *go*[w] *away*.
Words like *flower*, *power*, *tower*, *bowel*, *towel* are generally pronounced as one syllable, with no [w] sound in the middle—[flaə], [paə], etc.

PRACTICE

A.

(a)

		'wh'					
wind	Edward	what	white	wit	twice	quick	one
waves	Rowena	where	whisper	wet	twin	quite	once
water	blowing	why	whip	what	twain	queen	
world	Orwell	when	whining	wait	twelve	squash	
woods	wonderful	which	whether	white	between	squeeze	

silent 'w'

t(w)o	(w)hom	(w)hole	(w)rite	Chis(w)ick
(w)ho	(w)hose	s(w)ord	(w)rong	ans(w)er

(b)

[w]/[v] contrast	*[w]/[f] contrast*
wet / vet	weed / feed
wow / vow	white / fight
west / vest	wish / fish
wine / vine	warm / form

(c) We weave well at 'The Weavewell'. A well-woven 'Weavewell' weave wears well.
Oh, what a tangled web we weave, when first we practise to deceive.
We never miss the water till the well runs dry.
Wine, women and song.
All the world and his wife were there.
Weak as water.
Waste not, want not.

B. *Practise putting a [w] sound between a syllable ending in [uː], [əʊ] [aʊ], followed by another vowel. Remember, this happens even when the two syllables are in separate words.*

(a)

doing	do end	go in	The Plough and the Stars
going	do up	go out	Slough and Windsor
poetical	do answer	go away	thou art a fool

(b) Oh, I do admire your photo album. It's so organised.
Joe and Joanna were going to Amsterdam.
Who agreed to answer the radio advertisement?
Now I wonder how on earth we're going to plough our way through all this!

DIALOGUE 10. Rowena, are you awake?

EDWARD: Rowena! Are you awake?
ROWENA: What? Edward, what's wrong? What time is it?
EDWARD: Oh, about two o'clock.
ROWENA: In the *morning*? Oh, go away! What are you doing?
EDWARD: Come to the window, Rowena. Look—the whole world's white, there's a wicked wind blowing through Orwell Wood, whispering in the willows, whipping the water into waves, while over in the West . . .
ROWENA: Oh, waxing poetical! You *are* off your head! I always knew it! Why are you wearing your wellingtons?
EDWARD: I want to go out and wander in the woods. Come with me, Rowena! I can't wait to go walking in that wild and wonderful weather.
ROWENA: I wish you wouldn't wake me up at two in the morning to go on a wild-goose chase!
EDWARD: Oh, woman, woman! Stop *whining*! What a wet blanket you are!

11. [f], [v], [w]

Relative lip positions

PRACTICE

A. *[w]/[v]/[f] contrast*

wail	: veil	: fail
worst	: versed	: first
wheel	: veal	: feel
wane	: vein	: feign
wend	: vend	: fend
wire	: via	: fire
while	: vile	: file
wine	: vine	: fine
worn	: Vaughan	: fawn
weird	: veered	: feared

B. *Which is s/he saying?*

(a) Goodness, that aeroplane's fast! / vast!

(b) That was the first / worst thing she said.

(c) Go and see if they've sent the veal, / wheel, will you?

(d) Is that the fine / vine / wine you were telling me about?

C. *In each of the following groups, one word is more strongly stressed than the rest. Can you hear which it is? Is the word acting as a noun or an adjective? (Sometimes a noun takes the function of an adjective.)*
Mark all the stressed syllables and then put a line under the strongest stress in each group.

foreign visitors
Wednesday evening
Swedish representatives

watercress soup
white wine sauce
wide variety

fresh fruit soufflé
vanilla wafers
devilled soft roes

Answers: B. (a) fast (b) worst (c) veal (d) wine
C. The words with strongest stress are all nouns (but *not* ones playing at being adjectives!).

fóreign vísitors
Wédnesday évening
Swédish represéntatives

wátercress sóup
whíte wine sáuce
wíde varíety

frésh frúit sóufflé
vanílla wáfers
dévilled sóft róes

DIALOGUE 11. Twenty foreign visitors

EVELYN: What are you giving your foreign visitors on Wednesday evening, Winnie? How many—twelve, is it?

WINNIE: Twenty. Twelve of William's Swedish representatives, eight of them with wives.

EVELYN: And what will you feed them on?

WINNIE: Well, we'll start with watercress soup, then fish in a white wine sauce flavoured with fennel and chives, followed by stuffed veal served with cauliflower and . . . oh, a very wide variety of vegetables.

EVELYN: Mmm. My mouth's watering!

WINNIE: For sweet we'll have fresh fruit soufflé covered with walnuts. And lots of whipped cream, of course, and vanilla wafers. And we'll finish with devilled soft roes.

EVELYN: And finally coffee? What a feast! I wish I was going to be with you!

12. [ə] ('shwa'—the only sound that has a name) among, sofa

This is a very important sound in English; though you might actually call it a non-sound. It is fully relaxed and very short. In fact, it is so short that it sometimes hardly exists at all!

It is the sound you have been making when you make the consonant sounds, for instance [p] and [b], audible. It is the sound you use for all the weak forms (see Units 30–32) (a boy, the girl, etc.) and for the unstressed syllables of so many words (police, contain, success). Try saying these words as if there were no vowel at all between the consonants of the unstressed syllable ([plíːs], [kntéɪn], [sksés]). With some combinations of consonants it is almost impossible not to make a slight sound, but if you concentrate [kɒ́nsntreɪt] on trying to eliminate the sound altogether, the most that will escape will be *shwa* and you will be overcoming the temptation to give the unstressed vowels their full value. When the unstressed syllable is an open one, i.e. at the end of a word with no following consonant sound and no linking with the next word (áctor [æktə], fínger [fɪŋgə], sófa [səʊfə]), it cannot, of course, be swallowed completely but is still very weak.

It is impossible in so short a space to give you all the spellings of syllables that are pronounced *shwa* [ə]. But here are a few general principles:

Before and/or after a strongly stressed syllable, especially the following spellings:

(a) **'a'** initial (abóut); final (chína)
-acy (légacy) -and (húsband) -ain (cúrtain) ant/-ce (impórtant/-ce)
-ard (víneyard) -graphy/-er (photógraphy/-er) -ham (Twíckenham)
-land (Éngland) -man (Nórman/húman)

(b) **'e'** in -el (párcel) -en (dózen) -ent (próvident) -ence/-se (síxpence/nońsense)
-er (áfter) -ment (góvernment)

(c) **'i'** in -ir (confirmátion)

(d) **'o'** especially in words ending in -ody (nóbody) -ogy (apólogy)
-oly (monópoly) -omy (ecónomy) -on (Dévon) -ony (hármony)
-ophy (philósophy) -or (áctor) -ory (híckory) -dom (kińgdom)
-some (hańdsome) -our (hárbour) -ford (Oxford) -folk (Nórfolk)
-don/-ton (Wímbledon/Bríghton)

'o' beginning: po- (polite) pro- (províde) com- (compláin) con- (contáin) and lots more two-syllable words in which the unstressed syllable contains the letter **'o'**.

(e) **'u'**: -um/-umn (máximum/aútumn) -us (circus) -ur (Sáturday)

(f) **Syllables spelt**: -tion (relátion) -ssion (pássion) -sion (vísion)
-cian (magícian) -ious (spácious) -ous (dańgerous, ridículous)
-ial (spécial, paŕtial) -ure (náture, préssure, ińjure, léisure)

(g) **Unstressed syllables on either side of a stressed one:**
advénture América amúsement forgótten permíssion
compóser narrátor perfórmance vacátion banána

(h) **All the 'weak forms'** that we shall come across in Units 30, 31 and 32.

(i) **Sometimes the unstressed syllable disappears altogether**, often for reasons of rhythm. Try to be aware of these as you listen:
cómfort [kʌmfət] *but* cómf(or)table [kʌmftəbʊl]
cáreful [keəfʊl] *but* cáref(u)lly [keəflɪ]
végetate [vedʒɪteɪt] *but* vég(e)table [vedʒtəbʊl]

Remember that 'shwa' is only used for unstressed syllables.

PRACTICE

A.

(a)

about	combine	potato	succession	actor
among	command	police	tradition	doctor
ago	confuse	propose	occasion	motor
water	theatre	extra	human	postman
danger	centre	sofa	woman	Englishman
driver	metre	china	German	gentleman
husband	England	curtain	dozen	student
company	Scotland	certain	written	entertainment
servant	Iceland	Britain	often	intelligent
lesson	adventure	generous	photographer	apology
bacon	future	ridiculous	stenographer	philology
cotton	pleasure	nervous	caligrapher	biology
thorough	Peterborough	St. Joan	Venus	cousin
borough	Edinburgh	St. Ives	asparagus	basin

(b) *The vanishing syllable.*

comf(or)table	caref(u)lly	list(e)ning	rest(au)rant	ord(i)nary
veg(e)table	practic(a)lly	lit(e)rature	cam(e)ra	extr(a)ord(i)n(a)ry
adm(i)rable	strawb(e)rry	med(i)c(i)ne	secret(a)ry	diff(e)rent

(c) A Doctor of Philosophy
A command performance
A picture of innocence
A baker's dozen

The Department of the Environment
The Iron Curtain
The Listening Library
The Garden of Eden

To bet your bottom dollar
To take your pleasures seriously

To harbour a grudge

Nature is the best healer
Nothing succeeds like success
Necessity is the mother of invention

A handsome husband—or ten thousand a year?
An Englishman's home is his castle
Here today, gone tomorrow
Never put off till tomorrow what you can do today
Never do today what you can get someone else to do tomorrow!

B. *Put a stress mark on the stressed syllables and underline those that are weakened to [ə] ('shwa').*

Twickenham	Addlestone	Brighton	Wimbledon	Norfolk
Bournemouth	Edinburgh	Oxford	Widecombe	Chester

How many more towns in Great Britain do you know that end in -ton, -don, -ham, -ford, -combe, -burgh (or -borough), etc.?

And how many 'shires' (pronounced [ʃə]), e.g. Devonshire?
N.B. In Scotland 'shire' is pronounced [ʃaɪə].

C. *Now put stress marks on the stressed syllables and underline the 'shwa' syllables in the names of these countries, and in the adjectives derived from them:*

Italy	Jordan	Brazil	Morocco	Japan	Belgium	Peru
Germany	Hungary	Canada	Russia	India	Argentina	Panama

D. *A rhyme . . .*

Rub-a-dub dub,
Three men in tub.
The butcher, the baker,
The candlestick-maker,
They all jumped over a rotten potater!

. . . and a riddle

As I was going to St Ives,
I met a man with seven wives.
Each wife had seven sacks;
Each sack had seven cats;
Each cat had seven kittens.
Kits, cats, sacks, wives—
How many were going to St Ives?

E. *How many of the characters in the dialogues in this book have names that contain 'shwa'? You'll have to listen to them to get the answers!*

Answers: B. Twíckenham, Áddlestone, Bríghton, Wímbledon, Nórfolk, Boúrnemouth, Édinburgh, Óxford, Wídecombe, Chéster

C. Ítaly/Itálian Jórdan/Jordánian Brazíl/Brazílian
Gérmany/Gérman Húngary/Hungárian Cánada/Canádian

Morócco/Moróccan Japán/Japanése Bélgium/Bélgian
Rússia/Rússian Índia/Índian Argentína/Argentínian

Perú/Perúvian
Panamá/Panamánian

D. Only one! *I* was going to St Ives when I *met* all the others—they were going the other way.

E. Peter, Tessa, Deirdre, Diana, Jeremy, Felicity, Oliver, Victor, Edward, Rowena, Christopher, Ezra, Anthony, Sheila, Patricia, Richard, Arthur, Father, Mother, Hanna, Jonathan, Elizabeth, Serena, Barnabas, Roger, Parker, Celia, Duncan, Cuthbert, Martha, Annabel, Rachel, Theresa, Second Bird Howard, Gentleman, Aaron, Piers, Robert, Sergeant, Policeman, Passer-by, Fisherman.

DIALOGUE 12. Comfort, culture or adventure?

CHRISTOPHER: Going anywhere different for your vacation, Theresa?

THERESA: Ah, that's a million dollar question, Christopher. Perhaps *you* can provide us with the decision. Edward demands his creature comforts—proper heating, constant hot water, comfortable beds, colour television . . .

CHRISTOPHER: What about you, Theresa? Or aren't you too particular?

THERESA: Normally, yes. And usually we combine the open air and exercise with a bit of culture. Last year, for instance, we covered the Cheltenham Festival. The year before, it was Edinburgh. Edward adores Scotland.

CHRISTOPHER: You fortunate characters! Are you complaining?

THERESA: No, but I long to go further afield—something more dangerous—and where the temperature's hotter!

CHRISTOPHER: I wonder if this would interest you. It arrived today. 'A Specialised Tour of Southern America for Photographers. Canoeing up the Amazon. Alligators. And other hazardous adventures.'

THERESA: Christopher, how marvellous! It sounds wonderful.

CHRISTOPHER: No creature comforts for Edward!

THERESA: Separate holidays are an excellent idea—occasionally! Edward can go to Scotland alone.

13. Sentence rhythm

In Unit 7 we discussed the stressing of certain syllables within individual words, ChinESE, compeTItion, POlitics, and so on. These stressed syllables are louder and higher and longer than the unstressed ones. In Unit 11 (Ex. C) we saw that both nouns and adjectives have stresses. Do all words have stress? Well, if you listen carefully to the dialogues you will notice that some words are swallowed almost completely. Which words? How does one know what to stress and what not to?

It's easiest to explain by imagining a situation: Jane has been invited to spend the weekend with Elizabeth in the depths of the country. She has to send a telegram to say when she is arriving, and she wants Elizabeth to meet her. Here's her telegram:

ARRIVING BANFORD STATION SATURDAY NOON. PLEASE MEET, LOVE JANE.

Both Jane and Elizabeth know the background, so the telegram contains *all the necessary information*. Originally Jane wrote a quick note, and then thought a telegram was safer. This is what she said in her note:

I shall be arriving at Banford Station on Saturday at noon. Please can you meet me? With love from Jane.

Now listen to the man in the Post Office reading the telegram, and then Jane reading the note she decided not to send.

Did you notice two things?

1. When Jane read her note, the only words you heard clearly were the information-carrying words that she put into the telegram (the 'telegram words') and, within those words, only the syllables that were stressed.
2. When the Post Office clerk read the telegram, he spaced the words so that the stresses came in a very regular beat. And when Jane read her note, the stresses came in the same regular pattern so that, in fact, though the note was so much longer than the telegram, *they both took the same amount of time to say out loud.*

Now listen to Jane and the clerk as they read their bits of paper in unison:

But what about all those words that Jane had to fit in between the 'telegram words'? Let's take a look at them:

I shall be . . . at . . . . . . on . . . at . . . . can you . . . me?
With . . . from . . . .

If we analyse them we find they are:

(a) pronouns (I/you/me),
(b) auxiliary and modal verbs, i.e. not main verbs (shall/be/can),
(c) prepositions (at/on/With/from).

To these we must add:

(d) articles (the/a/an),
(e) conjunctions (and/but, etc.).

So all these unimportant, non-'telegram words' have to be fitted in between the stresses, as well as the unstressed syllables of the 'telegram words' themselves.

How did Jane do it? Even before the first stress, the Post Office clerk had only one unstressed syllable; Jane had **four**:

I shall be arRIV-

The answer is that those four unstressed syllables came out as a rapid sort of mumble, like a muffled machine gun. This meant that the stressed syllables were still evenly spaced as she spoke. And this gave a rhythm, a sort of music, to her speech.

In real life we don't keep a regular beat throughout the whole of what we're saying; we alter the speed and rhythm from phrase to phrase. However, to begin with it's best to work at sentences, or even whole dialogues, as if they were all one single phrase and therefore being said at the same speed. We'll read Jane's note as if it was all one phrase. The stresses will therefore come at regular intervals of time all the way through. How many unstressed syllables are there between the stresses? (Here ˘ shows an unstressed syllable.)

> Ĭ shăll bĕ ăr**RI**vĭng ăt **BAN**fŏrd **STA**tiŏn ŏn **SAT**uřdaў ăt **NOON**. **PLEASE** căn yŏu **MEET** m̆e, Wĭth **LOVE** frŏm **JANE**

There is only **one** unstressed syllable between 'BAN-' and 'STA-' ('*ford*') and between 'LOVE' and 'JANE' ('*from*'), so let's take those to establish our speed—nice and slow to begin with—TUM ti TUM. There are **two** syllables between '-RI-' and 'BAN-', 'PLEASE' and 'MEET', 'MEET' and 'LOVE': so '*-ving at*', '*-tion on*', and '*me with*' must fit into the same time space as the single syllables '*-ford*' and '*from*'. They will therefore have to be said twice as fast. Remember, they must be regular, too—TUM ti ti TUM. Now '*-turday at*' has **three** syllables, so it will have to be said at three times the speed of '*-ford*', and '*from*'. '*I shall be a-* is **four** unstressed syllables in a row (you have to imagine that there was a stress immediately before them) so each of those syllables must be said at four times the speed of '*-ford*' and '*from*', and twice the speed of each syllable in the two-syllable groups.

Finally, between 'PLEASE' and 'MEET' there are **no** unstressed syllables at all. Do not speed up! These two stresses must still keep their distance. So what we do is hang on to the first word till the rhythm tells us that it's time to say the next: ('*ple-e-ease*') (see Unit 25).

Try saying the whole of Jane's note as TUM ti TUMS, keeping your TUMS at strictly regular intervals of time:

> ti ti ti ti TUM | ti ti TUM | ti TUM | ti ti TUM | ti ti ti TUM | TUM | ti ti TUM | ti ti TUM | ti TUM.

Practise it until you can do it at the same speed as the speaker on the tape, then try to put the words in on top of the TUM ti TUMS on the tape and finally see if you can say it with Jane as she reads the note out again.

Notice that in the dialogue, Chris speaks all the way through in a TUM ti TUM rhythm, Elise in a TUM ti ti TUM one. Until the whole thing comes naturally to you, try to keep the speed regular, even when the rhythms are different, as Chris and Elise do on the tape.

The rule to remember: 'Within each phrase, stresses come at regular intervals of time.'

PRACTICE

A.

(a) *Two nursery rhymes with very different rhythms:*

Jáck and Jíll
Went úp the híll
To fétch a páil of wá-tér.
Jáck fell dówn
And bróke his crówn
And Jíll came túmbling áf-tér.

(b) A fármer went trótting upón his grey máre,
Búmpety búmpety búmp (*pause*)
With his dáughter behínd him so rósy and fáir,
Lúmpety lúmpety lúmp.

B. *Here are three groups of numbers of different lengths on the paper, but which should take the same amount of time to say:*

(a)

twó twénty twó hundred	thrée thírty thrée hundred	foúr foŕty foúr hundred

(b) *three groups of words of similar difficulty:*

a a a de-	níce lóve-ly lí-cious and	rípe júicy móuth-wat(e)ring	péar mélon píneapple

(c) *and another three groups, rather more difficult:*

his his an out-	néw látest stánding contri-	boók's nóvel's a dis- bútion to con-	quíte tínct suc- témporary	góod céss lít(e)rature

C. *Which are the stressed syllables? When you've decided, read the passage aloud, exaggerating the stresses and trying to keep them at regular intervals of time. In real speech, as I have said, speed and rhythm vary from phrase to phrase. This exercise is just to get you into the habit of thinking in terms of rhythm and feeling it as you speak, so read the whole passage at the same speed and with strictly regular rhythm.*

'Excuse me—er—haven't we met before? Yes, I'm certain we have, I recognise your face. I'm never wrong. I'm terribly bad at names, but I never forget a face. Aren't you a friend of the Joneses—James and Isabel Jones? No? Oh, have I made you miss your bus? I'm *so* sorry. But I'm *sure* we've met before. I never forget a face.'

Answer: C. 'Excuśe mé—er—háven't we mét befoŕe? Yés, I'm cértain we havé, I récognísé your fáce. I'm néver wróng. I'm térribly bád at námes, but I never forgét a fáce. Áren't you a friend óf the Jóneses—Jámes and Ísabel Jónes? Nó? Óh, háve I máde you míss your bús? I'm *só* sórry. But I'm *súre* we've mét befóre. I néver forgét a fáce.

DIALOGUE 13: Elise's hair is green!

CHRIS: I líke your hát, Elíse.
ELISE: That iśn't my hát, it's my háir.
CHRIS: Your háir? You cán't have háir like thát. Elíse, it's brílliant gréen!
ELISE: Old wómen can dýe their hair blúe. There are plénty who paínt their nails réd.
CHRIS: That's nót the sáme at áll. They ońly stréss what náture meánt. Greén is . . . greén is . . . I cánnot fínd the wórds.
ELISE: Unnátural—is thát what you méan? An appéndix operátion is, tóo. And ás for transplánting a heárt . . . ! And I *lóve* all my émerald háir!
CHRIS: Whát does Péter thínk?
ELISE: Oh Chrístopher! Dídn't you knów? Why, *his* hair is púrple and réd!

14. [s] sue

This is a voiceless sound. Place the tip of your tongue between your teeth so that the teeth grip the sides of the tongue firmly. Now draw back the very tip and press it against the bottom teeth. There should now be a small passage over the top of the tongue through which air can pass straight from the lungs. Keep the lips spread and expel the air in a hissing sound.

PRACTICE

A.

(a)

seem	slow	serious	yes	most
soft	skin	sensible	miss	waste
Sam	sweet	sister	glass	ask
				[ks]
perhaps	nice	bicycle	scene	box
looks	city	agency	scent	accent
wants	cinema	Cyprus	science	succeed
silent 's'				
ai(s)le	i(s)land	Gro(s)venor	Carli(s)le	chassi(s)

(b) Better safe than sorry.
A lisping lass is good to kiss.
It's a silly goose that comes to a fox's sermon.
He who sups with the devil must use a long spoon.
I scream, you scream, we all scream for ice-cream.
Last but not least.
One swallow doesn't make a summer.

B. *Which is s/he saying?*

(a) I think Susie's rather sick. / thick.

(b) Is she going to sow / show those radishes?

(c) Did you say he'd made a pass? / path?

(d) I do believe I'm a little sinner. / thinner.

(e) B understands what I'm saying, but C / she doesn't.

C. *Mark the stresses on the following words before you listen to the tape:*

secure	literate	sensible	honest
insecure	illiterate	insensible	dishonest
suitable	possible	successful	sense
unsuitable	impossible	unsuccessful	nonsense

Answers: B. (a) sick (b) show (c) pass (d) thinner (e) C

C.

secúre	líterate	sénsible	hónest
insecúre	illíterate	insénsible	dishónest
súitable	póssible	succéssful	sénse
unsúitable	impóssible	unsuccéssful	nónsense

Did you remember *no* stress on a negative prefix, except the 'no' ones?

DIALOGUE 14. A sweet Siamese student

SAM: That Siamese student seems a nice sort of person.

STAN: Yes, serious, sensible—a bit insecure, perhaps. Eldest of six—the rest still at school.

SAM: I see her sister sometimes. I saw her yesterday.

STAN: Soft skin, silky voice, sleepy eyes, sort of slow, sexy smile.

SAM: Sounds like Siew Sang.

STAN: Yes. That's it—Siew Sang. She's so sweet.

SAM: Waxing ecstatic, Stan? I must say, I strongly disapprove of senior staff taking fancies to innocent students. You're supposed to be embracing serious linguistic research, not soft-skinned students! Most unsuitable. And silly, when you're just starting to make a success of this place . . .

STAN: For goodness' sake, Sam. Who says I'm smitten? The kid's sweet but still only 26. I shall be 60 in September!

15. [z] zoo

This, like its voiceless equivalent [s], is a *continuous* sound. There is no [d] or [t] before it. The lips and tongue are in the same position as for [s] but the vocal cords are vibrated, which will cause some tension in the tongue itself. The vibration should be very strongly felt.

PRACTICE

A.

(a)

			's' after long vowel		*plural or 3rd sing. 's' after voiced consonant*	
zoo	crazy	as	days	revise	things	leaves
zebra	horizon	was	close	windows	mouths	adds
zoology	puzzle	his	these	Thursday	hands	earns

[ɪz] '-es' after [s], [z], [ʃ], [tʃ], [ks], [dʒ]	*'x' [gz]*	*names*	*possessives [ɪz]*
misses	exams	Charles	Charles's
freezes	exact	Wales	Wales's
washes	exaggerate	James	James's
watches	exhausted	Dickens	the fox's
fixes	exist	the Joneses	Mr Hodge's
wages	exhibit	the Lyonses	Alice's

(b) *Practise lengthening the vowel.*

cats	bus	laps	fierce	east	Bruce
cads	buzz	labs	fears	eased	bruise

(c) She's as old as the hills.
It never rains but it pours.
If wishes were horses, then beggars would ride.
To cut off one's nose to spite one's face.
A miss is as good as a mile.
The end justifies the means.

B. *Which is s/he saying?*

(a) There seemed to be ice / eyes all around us.

(b) Do you want peace, / peas, or don't you?

(c) I can't take my eyes off your pretty niece. / knees.

(d) We raced across the fence. / fens.

(e) I'm afraid he prices / prizes his produce too highly.

C. *Without looking back at Unit 7, can you remember where the stress is on these words?*

zoology	theology	logical	physical	examination
zoologist	theologian	illogical	physician	anxious
zoological	theological	logistics	physicist	revision

Answers: B. (a) eyes (b) peace (c) knees (d) fens (e) prices
C. zoology theology logical physical examination
zoologist theologian illogical physician anxious
zoological theological logistics physicist revision

DIALOGUE 15. The zoology exam's on Thursday

EZRA: How's things these days, Lizzie?
LIZZIE: I'm exhausted. Revising for the zoology exam!
EZRA: You've got bags under your eyes, Lizzie. Take it easy!
LIZZIE: It's all very well for you to advise, Ezra, but I'm going crazy. One of those miserable Zeno boys, two houses down, plays his transistor as if he was as far away as Mars!
EZRA: Boys will be boys. These days everyone plays transistors.
LIZZIE: But he refuses to close the windows!
EZRA: Then close your ears to the noise, Lizzie. One learns to ignore these things, as if they didn't exist.
LIZZIE: Please, Ezra. The exam's on Thursday.
EZRA: And today's Tuesday! That only leaves two days! You'd better get busy, Lizzie!

16. [ʃ] ship, wash

For this sound the tongue is pulled further back than for [s] and the tip of the tongue is lifted to midway between the teeth. If you purse your lips as you did for [w], this will help initially, though later you may not find it necessary. Do it this way until you are sure that you hear and feel the difference between [s] and [ʃ]. Start with the tip of the tongue actually between your teeth. Draw it back slowly till you are saying [s], then further still. You should be able both to hear and to feel the change in the quality of the sound.

PRACTICE

A.

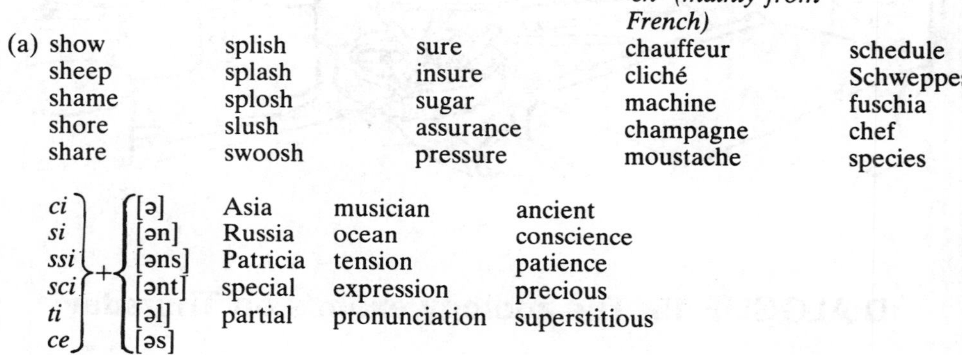

(a)

			'ch' (mainly from French)	
show	splish	sure	chauffeur	schedule
sheep	splash	insure	cliché	Schweppes
shame	splosh	sugar	machine	fuschia
shore	slush	assurance	champagne	chef
share	swoosh	pressure	moustache	species

ci	[ə]	Asia	musician	ancient
si	[ən]	Russia	ocean	conscience
ssi +	[əns]	Patricia	tension	patience
sci	[ənt]	special	expression	precious
ti	[əl]	partial	pronunciation	superstitious
ce	[əs]			

(b) Share and share alike.
Ship to shore communication.
She sells sea shells on the sea shore.
Short and sweet—and the shorter the sweeter.

To manage on a shoestring.

Shear your sheep in May,
You shear them all away.

B. *What order is s/he saying these in?*

(a) save shave	(b) mess mesh	(c) sip ship	(d) sock shock	(e) crust crushed
(f) sea she	(g) puss push	(h) sort short	(i) person Persian	(j) fist fished

C. 'She speaks English and Danish and Polish and Flemish . . .' *Can you go on?* (*If you are in a whole class this can be done as a game, with each person repeating the whole list and adding one more language.*)

Answers: B. (a) shave save (b) mess mesh (c) ship sip (d) shock sock (e) crust crushed (f) she sea (g) push puss (h) sort short (i) Persian person (j) fist fished

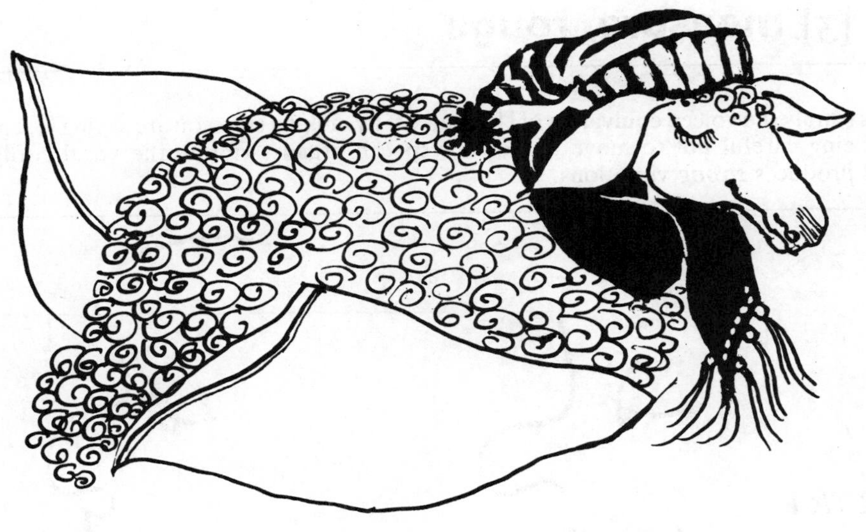

DIALOGUE 16. Are you sure you said *sheep*?

SHEILA: 'Tricia, come and I'll show you my sheep.
PATRICIA: Your *sheep*? Sheila, *what* sheep?
SHEILA: *My* sheep.
PATRICIA: Are you sure you said *sheep*?
SHEILA: Shh, don't shout. Of course I'm sure I said sheep. She's here in the shed. Isn't she sweet? She was washed up on the shore at Shale Marsh.
PATRICIA: What a shame! Is it unconscious?
SHEILA: She's a *she*. I shall call her Sheba. I should think she's suffering from shock.
PATRICIA: Do you think she was pushed off that Persian ship? Oh Sheila, she's shivering.
SHEILA: My precious! She shall have a soft cushion and my cashmere shawl!
PATRICIA: She's rather special, isn't she? Sheila, I wish—oh, I do wish we could *share* her!

17. [ʒ] measure, rouge

This is simply the voiced equivalent of [ʃ]. Start off by making sure you are saying [ʃ] correctly and, being careful not to move any of our speech organs, vibrate the vocal cords. This sound produces *strong* vibrations.

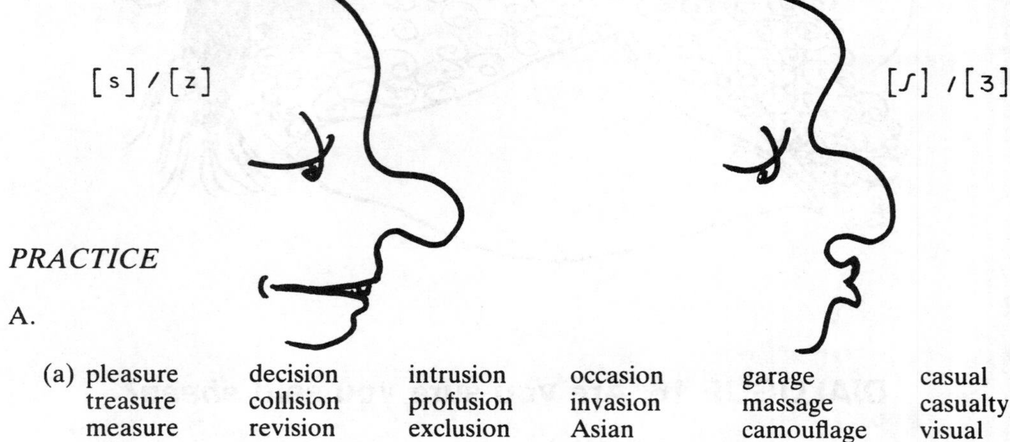

PRACTICE

A.

(a)

pleasure	decision	intrusion	occasion	garage	casual
treasure	collision	profusion	invasion	massage	casualty
measure	revision	exclusion	Asian	camouflage	visual
leisure	precision	delusion	evasion	prestige	usual
enclosure	television	confusion	persuasion	beige	usually

(b) Confusion worse confounded. Stolen pleasures are sweetest.
Your old men shall dream dreams, your young men shall see visions.
That man is richest whose pleasures are the cheapest.

B. *Which is s/he saying?*

(a) I do admire your great composer. / composure.

(b) Your baize / beige tablecloth's perfect for playing bridge.

(c) Excuse me, is this Aden? / Asian?

(d) Were you talking about the discovery of nuclear fission? / new clear vision?

C. *Listen to the dialogue. Mark the stressed syllables in these words.*

decision	television	occasion	intrusion
pleasure	conversation	leisure	unusual
revision	allusion	casually	treasure

Answers: B. (a) composer (b) beige (c) Asian (d) nuclear fission
C. That was easy, wasn't it, even without the tape? Did you remember that the stress always falls on the syllable before: [ʒə] (le*i*sure), [ʒn] (*v*ision), [ʒl] (*u*sual), and [ʒn] (conver*sa*tion)?

decísion	televísion	occásion	intrúsion
pléasure	conversátion	léisure	unúsual
revísion	allúsion	cásually	tréasure

DIALOGUE 17. The great decision

JACQUES: I have made a great decision, Jean. I have bought a television.

JEAN: You? Jacques, on how many occasions have you told me that television was an intrusion into the privacy of the house, that it destroyed the pleasures of conversation, that people no longer know how to make use of their leisure . . .

JACQUES: I know, I know. And it's unusual for me to suffer a revision of thought, but on this occasion . . .

JEAN: Where is this treasure?

JACQUES: Hidden in the garage. Please make no allusion to it. I shall tell the family casually, as if there were nothing unusual in my buying a television.

JEAN: After years of derision—I hope you will not be disillusioned by your television.

18. [tʃ] chin, watch

This is actually a combination of two sounds, but they are produced so close that they count as one. The [t] is not aspirated, but slides straight on to the [ʃ], after which the air is expelled. Because there are two sounds, however close, it is impossible to hang on to the sound as one can with [f] or [s], for example. You *can* hold on to the [ʃ] part, but if you want to keep saying the whole phoneme, you have to break off and start again, rather like a steam engine: [tʃ-tʃ-tʃ].

PRACTICE

A.

(a) *Make the sound of a train, 'TCHER tcher tcher tcher', in the rhythm 'ONE two three four' over and over again as many times as you like. Then change the vowel: 'TCHOO tchoo tchoo tchoo', 'TCHI tchi tchi tchi', 'TCHA tcha tcha tcha', etc., repeating each new set several times.*

(b)

Charles	much	butcher	capture	question	'cello
change	switch	teacher	adventure	suggestion	concerto
choose	watch	merchant	furniture	indigestion	righteous
chips	branch	kitchen	future	Christian	fortunate
cheese	lunch	chicken	century	combustion	mixture

(c) Catch as catch can.
Such a charming child!
Children are poor men's riches.
You scratch my back, I'll scratch yours.
Don't count your chickens before they're hatched.
How much wood would a woodchuck chuck, if a woodchuck could chuck wood?

B. *One word in each of these sentences turns the whole sentence into nonsense. Which are the words? And what* **ought** *they to be?*

(a)
(b)
(c)
(d)
(e)
(f)

C. *Syllable stress*

Can you do these **before** *you listen to the dialogue? Then listen and check before you look at the answers.*

recapture	suggest	future	another	nature
direction	childhood	further	chocolate	adventure
different	century	arrival	adjourn	fortune
question	channel	actually	departure	kitchen

Answers: B. (a) They burnt the poor *wits* (witch) at the stake.
(b) All the *catch* (cats) in the neighbourhood chased the rats.
(c) It was a very boring *mats* (match).
(d) What's a *whats* (watch) in Spanish?
(e) His beard hides his weak *shin* (chin).
(f) I shall never let the blacksmith *chew* (shoe) my horse again.

C.

recapture	suggest	future	another	nature
direction	childhood	further	chocolate	adventure
different	century	arrival	adjourn	fortune
question	channel	actually	departure	kitchen

DIALOGUE 18. Life is a question of choice—or chance?

CHARLES: If you could recapture your childhood, Richard, would you change much?

RICHARD: Life is a sort of arch. Arrival to departure. You can't switch direction, Charles. Each century brings changes but actually, Nature doesn't change.

CHARLES: But you can reach different decisions. With television, you can choose which channel to watch, switch to another picture. You could catch a different train. Given the chance, Richard, would *you* change trains?

RICHARD: Life is a rich adventure and largely a question of chance. You don't choose your future as you choose a chocolate or a piece of cheese.

CHARLES: But, Richard, you *do* choose. You forge your own fortune—a.butcher? a 'cellist? a teacher? a merchant? Each choice suggests a further choice—*which* tree, *which* branch, *which* twig?

RICHARD: Let's adjourn to the kitchen for chicken and chips. No choice for lunch, you see, Charles!

CHARLES: But *you* actually *chose* chicken and chips! Chops would have been much cheaper!

19. [dʒ] jump, bridge

This is the voiced equivalent of [tʃ]. Try not to let any air escape on either sound. If anything, feel as if you are pushing the air back into your lungs. It is almost impossible to voice one sound without voicing the other, so make sure the [d] is properly pronounced and slide quickly on to the [ʒ].

PRACTICE

A.

(a) jaw, jar, Joe; jeans, just, job; pyjamas, injection, adjourn; gin, ginger, giraffe; George, edge, exchange

digestion, surgery, gently; village, cabbage, cottage; register, religion, engine; N.B.: margarine, procedure, soldier

(b) Change the subject.
The English language.
Sister Susie sewing shirts for soldiers.
Imagine an imaginary menagerie manager managing an imaginary menagerie.
Judge not, lest you be judged.
Be just before you are generous.

B. *Each of the following words contains one of the sounds [s], [z], [ʃ], [ʒ], [tʃ] or [dʒ]. Can you put the correct symbol by each word?*

(a) chew [ ] zoo [ ] shoe [ ]
(b) major [ ] nature [ ] laser [ ]
(c) east [ ] eased [ ] each [ ]
(d) large [ ] marsh [ ] march [ ]
(e) sheep [ ] cheap [ ] jeep [ ]
(f) rich [ ] ridge [ ]
(g) leisure [ ] ledger [ ]
(h) recent [ ] reasoned [ ]
(i) Tricia [ ] treasure [ ]
(j) vision [ ] pigeon [ ]

C. *Which is s/he saying?*

(a) The crowd cheered / jeered when he announced the results.
(b) English food makes people choke / joke all the time.
(c) He is the only chairman / German who has managed to keep the meeting short.
(d) That's a very fine-looking sheep / jeep you have there.
(e) I shall have to cash / cadge £5—I haven't got a bean.

D. *Mark the stress*

exchange, pyjamas, injuries, register
religion, procedure, adjourn, surgery
sandwich, orange juice, indigestion, generous
adjusting, engine, soldier, imagine
damaged, suggest, injection, syringe

Answers: B. (a) [tʃ] [z] [ʃ] (b) [dʒ] [tʃ] [z] (c) [s] [z] [tʃ] (d) [dʒ] [ʃ] [tʃ] (e) [ʃ] [tʃ] [dʒ]
(f) [tʃ] [dʒ] (g) [ʒ] [dʒ] (h) [s] [z] (i) [ʃ] [ʒ] (j) [ʒ] [dʒ]

C. (a) jeered (b) choke (c) chairman (d) jeep (e) cadge

D. exchánge, pyjámas, ínjuries, régister; relígion, procédure, adjóurn, súrgery; sándwich, órange júice, indigéstion, génerous; adjústing, éngine, sóldier, imágine; dámaged, suggést, injéction, sýringe

DIALOGUE 19. George's jaw

Dr Jones: Ah, George, jolly good. Just exchange your jacket and jeans for these pyjamas, while I jot down your injuries in my register. Age, religion, that's the usual procedure.

George: Well, Doctor Jones, I was just driving over the bridge on the edge of the village . . .

Dr Jones: Half a jiffy. Let's adjourn to the surgery. I've got a large sandwich and a jar of orange juice in the fridge. Join me?

George: Jeepers! My indigestion . . . and my jaw! I shan't manage . . .

Dr Jones: A generous measure of gin—just the job!

George: It's my jaw, Doctor. I was on the bridge at the edge of the village. I was just adjusting the engine when this soldier jumped out of the hedge . . .

Dr Jones: Imagine! He damaged your jaw, did he? I suggest an injection into the joint. Just a jiffy. I'll change the syringe.

George: Oh jeepers! Gently, Dr Jones!

20. Linking

In English we talk, not in individual words, but in groups of words, or phrases. Thus 'Good afternoon' is said without a break, as if it were one word. Similarly, 'What's it all about?' or 'I don't understand'. If you break the phrase—'I don't . . . understand'—this gives special emphasis to the word after the pause, because you have interrupted the rhythm and kept the listener in suspense.
There are a number of aids that help us maintain the fluency of the rhythm. One of these devices is *Linking*.
Within a phrase, and often between adjoining phrases, too, if a word begins with a vowel, the consonant at the end of the preceding word is joined to it (I'm talking of sound, not spelling):

Thi⌊si⌊sit   A⌊napple   Fu⌊llo⌊fink

When you practise, pause *before* the last sound in the first word and say this last sound as if it were the *first* sound of the next word:

thi si zit   a napple   fu lo vink

or, hold on to the last sound of the first word till you're ready to start the next:

[ðɪsssɪzzzɪt]   [ənnnæpʊl]   [fʊlllәvvɪnk]

If the end of one word and the beginning of the next are both vowel sounds, you insert a consonant sounds as we saw in Unit 10. After [ʊ], [u:], [aʊ] you add [w], after [ɪ], [i:] you add [j]. [eɪ], [ɑɪ] and [ɔɪ] already have the [j] sound, which simply has to be strengthened a little. Before a vowel sound, weak forms become strong, i.e. 'the' is pronounced [ði:], 'to' [tu:]. 'A' has a special form, 'an' [ən].
In the short answers 'Yes, I am', 'No, I'm not', etc., you link across the comma as if it didn't exist: 'Yes‿I‿am', 'No‿I'm not'.

N.B. A vowel does not necessarily have a vowel sound. Words like 'union', 'university', etc., actually begin with a [j] sound; 'one' begins with a [w] sound.
Note also that initial 'h' is very often dropped so that you have to link with the vowel that follows.

PRACTICE

A.

(a) *Plain linking*	size eight	an apple	this orange	don't ask
	sit up	stop it	tell Alfred	I can explain
(b) *Adding [j]*	the animal	silly idiot!	try it on	say it again
	the answer	pretty awful	buy another	stay a while
(c) *Adding [w]*	to explain	you answer	so empty	go and see
	two and a half	I'm too upset	No, I didn't	Oh, all right

(d) Often after an 'a' you will hear an 'r' sound:
Anna^r and the King   Celia^r and Chris   Sheila^r and Patricia

B. *Practice in sentences.*

There's an elephant on top of the aeroplane!
John says he'll take out (h)is own appendix—it's such an easy operation.
We ate a banana an(d) an orange. So did Eva an(d) I.
He wants to have (h)is cake an(d) eat it.
This exercise is absolutely impossible, isn't it?

DIALOGUE 20. A job in Abadan

ERIC: Hullo,‿Anthony. Got‿a job yet?
ANTHONY: Well,‿I've just been‿up to‿Aylesbury for‿an‿interview.
ERIC: Oh? Was‿it‿interesting?
ANTHONY: Yes.‿An‿international‿oil company with‿interests‿in most‿of the‿eastern countries. Someone to‿organise‿an‿office they're‿opening‿up‿in‿Abadan.
ERIC: I‿imagine you'll have to brush up your‿Arabic‿again.
ANTHONY: Oh,‿I can‿express myself‿in‿Arabic‿all right. And‿I‿understand most‿other Middle‿Eastern languages. It's‿an‿exciting‿opportunity. They‿actually‿offered‿it to me‿outright.
ERIC: If‿I may‿express‿an‿unbiased‿opinion . . .
ANTHONY: Sorry,‿Eric.‿I've‿already‿accepted.

21. [θ] think, month

Put your tongue between your teeth, open your mouth *just* a little, take a deep breath and blow out the air, being careful not to let your tongue move from its position. Listen to yourself carefully as you say it and be *very* careful never to substitute [t] or [z].

PRACTICE

A.

(a)

thin	thumb	Thursday	three	throat
think	thump	theatre	throw	thrift
thing	thud	thousand	through	throttle
bath	fifth	healthy	strength	birthday
earth	sixth	wealthy	length	arithmetic
fourth	eighth	filthy	month	thirtieth

(b) *Words not to be confused. Make sure you are making the correct consonant sound in each word.*

thin	thank	thick	thigh	pith
tin	tank	tick	tie	pit
sin	sank	sick	sigh	piss
shin	shank	chic	shy	pish
thin	thirst	thought	threat	three
fin	first	fought	fret	free

(c) Through thick and thin.
Set a thief to catch a thief.
They're as thick as thieves.
'My feet had run through thrice a thousand years.'
If a thing's worth doing, it's worth doing well.
Truth and roses have thorns.
Thirty days hath September.

B. *Pronounce aloud*

3; 33; 333; 3,333; 33,333.

C. *Stress in compound nouns.*

In most of the 'noun–adjective' groups of words that we have looked at, both the noun and the adjective have stress, but the noun more than the adjective (foreign vísitors, wide varíety). There is, however, a group of words in which it may seem as if the adjective has the main stress (a dáncing master, a gréenfly). In fact, these are not adjective–noun combinations but *compound nouns*, often written with a hyphen or even as one word:

A dancing máster — a master who is dancing (adjective-noun)
A dáncing master — a master who teaches dancing (compound noun)

Practise saying these compounds, exaggerating the stress on the first word:

ténnis racquet	políce station	bús conductor
wríting paper	wálking stick	péncil sharpener

Then practise making the distinction between these pairs:

A black bírd : a bláckbird a blue bóttle : a blúebottle
a green flý : a gréenfly a leather jácket : a léatherjacket

DIALOGUE 21. My birthday's on Thursday

RUTH: It's my birthday on Thursday. My sixth birthday.

ARTHUR: My seventh birthday's on the 13th of next month, so I'm—let me think—333 days older than you, Ruth.

RUTH: Do you always put your thumb in your mouth when you're doing arithmetic, Arthur?

ARTHUR: My tooth's loose, Ruth. See? I like maths. I came fourth out of 33. My father's a mathematician.

RUTH: My father's an author. He writes for the theatre. We're very wealthy. When I'm 30 I'll have a thousand pounds.

ARTHUR: *I'm* going to be an Olympic athlete. I may be thin but Mr Smith says I've got the strength of three. Watch me. I'll throw this thing the length of the path.

RUTH: Oh Arthur! You've thrown earth all over us both. I'm filthy! Now they'll make me have a bath!

22. [ð] then, breathe

This is the voiced pair to [θ]. You will find that the effort of voicing presses your tongue a little further forward, pushing it harder against the teeth.

PRACTICE

A.

(a) *Notice the different vowel sounds:*

[ʌ]	brother	[ɒ]	bother	[e]	heather	tether	[iː]	heathen
	mother				weather	whether		breathing
	other				leather	together		
	another				feather			

[ɑː]	father	[eɪ]	bather	[æ]	gather	[aɪ]	either	*or* [iː]	either
	rather		lathe				neither		neither

(b) (i) *voiceless final 'th', voiced if followed by 'e', 'y', 's'*

teeth	north	mouth	wreath	worth
teethe	northern	mouths	wreathes	worthy

(ii) but *both voiceless in these nouns and the adjectives formed from them*

wealth	health	filth	length	tooth
wealthy	healthy	filthy	lengthy	toothy

(iii) *note the changed vowel sound in the following:*

[ɑː]	bath	[ɒ]	cloths	[e]	breath	[aʊ]	south	[ɒ]	moth
[eɪ]	bathe	[əʊ]	clothes	[iː]	breathe	[ʌ]	southern	[ʌ]	mother

(c) Birds of a feather flock together.
He that speaks, sows, and he that holds his peace, gathers.

'This above all—to thine own self be true,
And it must follow, as the night the day,
Thou canst not then be false to any man.'

B. *Fill in the gaps.*
(a) . . . . and sisters have I none, but . . . . man's . . . . is my . . . . son.
(b) I'd . . . . in a . . . . sea . . . . wear . . . . and a . . . . be.
(c) My younger . . . . is . . . . . . When he opens his . . . . you can see . . . . I don't . . . . he's . . . . about. My . . . . don't . . . . . gone off . . . . for a . . . . , leaving my . . . . to . . . . my younger . . . . .

Answers: B. (a) Brothers and sisters have I none, but that man's father is my father's son. (Can you work out who 'that man' is?)
(b) I'd rather bathe in a southern sea than wear thick clothes and a northerner be.
(c) My younger brother is teething. When he opens his mouth you can see three teeth. I don't think he's worth bothering about. My other brothers don't either. They've gone off together for a bathe, leaving my mother to bath my younger brother.

DIALOGUE 22. I'd rather be a mother than a father

FATHER: Where are the others?
MOTHER: They've gone bathing. Heather and her brother called for them.
FATHER: Heather Feather?
MOTHER: No, the other Heather—Heather Mather. I told them to stay together, and not to go further than Northern Cove.
FATHER: Why didn't you go with them?
MOTHER: I'd rather get on with the ironing without them.
FATHER: In this weather? There's a southerly breeze. One can hardly breathe indoors.
MOTHER: Go and have a bathe, then.
FATHER: Another bathe? I can't be bothered. I'll go with you, though.
MOTHER: But all these clothes . . . who'd be a mother!
FATHER: I'd rather be a mother than a father! All those hungry mouths!

23. [h] him

This is a very easy sound to produce but one which a lot of people find very difficult to attach to other sounds. To make it, simply open your mouth and push air up and out straight from the lungs. To produce it several times in succession, imagine that you have been running and are out of breath, or you are a dog panting. The problem in ordinary speech is to have sufficient breath in your lungs to expel at every [h]. Practise controlling the amount of air you expel so that you always have some in reserve.
Do not use this sound for linking.

PRACTICE

A.

(a)

hip	hill	his	hit	hum
hop	hell	horse	hut	home
heap	heel	house	heat	harm
hoop	hall	Hess	hate	ham

(b)

			silent 'h'		
perhaps	coathanger	who	(h)eir	r(h)ubarb	fore(h)ead
behave	upholstery	whom	(h)our	r(h)yme	shep(h)erd
behind	disheartened	whose	(h)onest	r(h)ythm	sil(h)ouette
unhappy	upheld	whole	(h)onour	ex(h)aust	Birming(h)am
inhuman	penthouse	whooping cough	ve(h)icle	ex(h)ibition	Blen(h)eim

(c) Handsome is as handsome does.
Come hell or high water.
He that has ears to hear let him hear.
Cold hands, warm heart.
Heaven helps him who helps himself.
He that has an ill name is half hanged.
In Hertford, Hereford and Hampshire, hurricanes hardly ever happen.
It's not the hopping over hedges that hurts the horses' hooves; it's the hammer, hammer, hammer on the hard high road.

B. *One word in each of these sentences turns it into nonsense. Which words are they?*

(a) (c) (e)
(b) (d) (f)

C. *Can you remember the syllable stress in these words without looking back?*

explain	post office	afternoon	director
radiator	hotel	extravagant	concentrate
concentration	market square	advise	disapproval
Arabic	Chinese	materialistic	phonology
unsuccessful	exciting	opportunity	decision

Answers: B. (a) He's head over *eels* (heels) in love.
(b) Are you going to clip the *hedge* (edge) of the lawn?
(c) I can't *ear* (hear) you very well.
(d) Because the enemy had left them *unarmed* (unharmed) they put down their weapons.
(e) It may be what you like, but is it *heart* (art)?
(f) The prince is *hair* (heir) to the throne.

C.

expláin	póst office	afternóon	diréctor
rádiator	hotél	extrávagant	cóncentrate
concentrátion	market squáre	advíse	disappróval
Árabic	Chinése	materialístic	phonólogy
unsuccéssful	excíting	opportúnity	decísion

DIALOGUE 23. Happy honeymoon

HAZEL: Hullo, Hanna. Have you heard about Hilda and Harry?
HANNA: Hilda and Harry Hall? They're on their honeymoon in Honolulu.
HAZEL: Yes, the Happy Holiday Hotel. But apparently they had the most hideous row.
HANNA: Hilda and her husband? Handsome Harry?
HAZEL: My dear, haven't you *heard*? He held her by the hair and hit her on the head with a hammer.
HANNA: What inhuman behaviour! I hope she's not badly hurt?
HAZEL: Heavens, yes! *Horribly!* He hurried her to the hospital—you know how Hilda hates hospitals.
HANNA: But how did it happen?
HAZEL: He *says* it was the heat that went to his head!

24. [ŋ] singer, thing

To make the [ŋ] sound, start with the mouth slightly open. Then breathe through the nose. If you have a mirror in front of you, you will see that the back of the tongue rises and the soft palate comes down to meet it, effectively blocking off the passage of air to the mouth. Now vibrate the vocal cords so that you produce a sound. That sound will be [ŋ]. To produce [ŋk], you release the barrier at the back of the mouth immediately after the [ŋ] so that the air now escapes through the mouth in the [k] sound. [ŋg] is formed in the same way, only the second sound is voiced and hardly any air escapes through the mouth.

PRACTICE

A. *[ŋ] (no [g] sound)*

(a)

sing	bring	ding	ring	ting	young/among
sang	bang	dang	rang	tang	
sung	bung	dung	rung	tongue	harangue/meringue
song	belong	dong	wrong	tong	

(b) *All the present participles ('we're singing') and gerunds ('I like talking')*

stretching	sitting	calling	tinkling
winding	watching	darkening	beginning
spreading	weeping	ringing	getting

(c) *These '-nger' words (N.B. all derived from verbs ending in '-ng')*

singer	ringer	coathanger
bringer	banger	hanger-on

B. *[ŋk]*

(a) *Here are just a few of the many words that end in [ŋk]. A good exercise is to go through the alphabet, thinking of all the possible combinations of letters and sounds, and then look them up in the dictionary to see if they exist, e.g. bink (no), brink and blink (yes).*

ink	pink	bank	sank	bunk	monk
drink	think	rank	stank	drunk	punk
mink	zinc	drank	thank	junk	trunk

(b) *In the middle of a word. Despite spelling these are all pronounced [ŋk].*

ankle	Manx	anchor	length	gangster
uncle	anxious	conquer	strength	([g] *becomes* [k] *because of following voiceless consonant)*
tinkle	han(d)kerchief	banquet	amongst	

C. *[ŋg]*

(a) *before:*
'a': kangaroo, nightingale, Hungary, Bengal, engage.
'o': Mongolia, mango, tango, angostura.
'u': singular, angular, fungus, language, penguin.
'l' : England, English and words that end in '-le': angle, single, jungle, etc.
'r' : congratulate, hungry, angry, mongrel.

(b) *some words before '-er' (N.B.* **not** *derived from verbs)*
e.g. finger, linger, hunger, conger eel, fishmonger, ironmonger

(c) *comparatives and superlatives of the three adjectives* long, strong, young:

long	strong	young
longer	stronger	younger
longest	strongest	youngest

DIALOGUE 24. A king and a song

INGRID: There once was a king—

MUNGO: King of England?

INGRID: No. This king's kingdom was far-flung, stretching along the banks of every winding river, spreading into all the angles of the world.

MUNGO: He must have been a very strong king. The strongest! Did *everything* belong to him?

INGRID: Almost everything. One evening he was sitting on the bank of his longest river, watching the sun sink behind the weeping willows—

MUNGO: And the nightingales calling from the darkening branches.

INGRID: Only they weren't nightingales. They were two monks ringing a tinkling bell, singing a sad lingering song in a strange tongue no longer known among the younger subjects of his far-flung kingdom.

MUNGO: It's beginning to be interesting. But I'm getting hungry. Can you bring me something to eat and drink, do you think, Ingrid?

25. More rhythm: consecutive stresses

Most of the time, in English speech, stressed syllables are separated by one or more unstressed ones. But every now and then there will be two stressed syllables, one straight after the other. There was a pair in Jane's telegram in Unit 13. 'PLEASE MEET', she wrote, and when the Post Office clerk read it, he had to hang on to the first word until it was time, strictly in accordance with the rhythm, to move on to the next. You will have done the same thing in the third and sixth lines of 'Jack and Jill':

. . . To fétch a páil of wá-tér. . . . And Jíll came túmbling áf-tér.

In ordinary speech, 'water' and 'after' each have only one stressed syllable, but rhythm overrides everything, especially in nursery rhymes, and so we have to say: 'wá-a-a-tér'.

If, when you were doing Exercise B of Unit 13, you repeated the groups of phrases several times without a break, you will have found yourself saying 'a delicious and mouth-watering pineapple', followed immediately by 'a nice ripe pear'—in fact, doing exactly what we're going to concentrate on in this unit.

Note that if you are holding on to an open vowel ('a grey horse') or a vowel before a voiced consonant ('a beige carpet'), you can lengthen the vowel sound almost indefinitely. However, if the vowel is followed by a voiceless consonant sound and therefore must be short, either

(a) you will have to lengthen the consonant sound: 'a nice-ce-ce person',

or (b) if the consonant sound is not one of those that can be continued indefinitely ([f], [s], [ʃ], etc.) but a 'plosive' ([p], [t], [k], etc.), you will get your speech organs in position to say the sound and only let go when the rhythm tells you to ('take two', 'top teeth').

PRACTICE

A. *Two consecutive stresses.*

loń́g wálk	táll mán	blúe ský	gréen gráss	bláck cát
brówn dóg	bríght sún	máin róad	frésh frúit	whóle cáke

B. *Now try the same pairs of words, this time in sentences.* In each sentence there should be at least one stressed syllable, apart from the two consecutive ones. Before you begin, decide which syllables you are going to stress. Then repeat each sentence at least twice, slowly at first and then a little faster.

She wént for a lóng wálk.
I've bought a brown dog.
He's looking for a tall man.
I love the bright sun.
What a wonderful blue sky.

We'll drive by the main road.
Let's sit on the green grass.
You must eat some fresh fruit.
A pretty little black cat.
They finished the whole cake.

C. *Go through the sentences again, stressing* ***only*** *the two consecutive stressed syllables:*

Wĕ weňt fŏr ă loń́g wálk.
I'v̆e boŭght ă brówn dóg.

Unless you can say the unstressed words very fast you will probably have to slow the two stressed ones down quite a lot.

DIALOGUE 25. All dressed up like a dog's dinner

SAM: Jáck, for Péte's sáke! Whó's thát gírl áll dréssed úp like a dóg's dínner—réd hát, réd dréss, réd glóves—áh! but whát's thís? Blúe shóes!

JACK: Táke thát back, Sám Bóyd. Dóg's dínner indéed!

SAM: You're quíte ríght! Mý dóg hátes ráw méat! He'd have tén fíts if I gáve him a réd méss like thát for dínner!

JACK: It's her bést dréss. To impréss *yóu*, you rúde créature! She's swéet, rích, cléver—*ánd* a góod cóok!

SAM: Lórd sáve us, the mán's mád! Dón't sáy you're in lóve with the réd maíden?

JACK: Yés, Sám. Í ám. Whát's móre—we're engáged. Thís tíme néxt wéek we'll be mán and wífe.

SAM: I díd réally put my bíg fóot in it, dídn't I? All I can sáy nów is—góod lúck, óld mán!

26. [l] lace/sail

Lay the front part of your tongue along the alveolar ridge, with the tip of the tongue touching the gums just where the teeth join them. Contract the tongue, drawing in the sides so that air can pass on either side. If you suck in air, you will feel it on the sides of your tongue. Now push the air out of your mouth, at the same time vibrating your vocal cords so that you produce a **voiced** sound. There are, in fact, two [l] sounds in English, but they are not phonemic, i.e. it makes no difference to meaning which one you use. The [l] you have just made (the 'clear' [l]) occurs before a vowel (like, lost, sailing, hollow). The other [l] sound (the 'dark' [ɫ]) occurs before a consonant sound (called, build) or at the end of a word (full, middle, chapel). To make the dark [ɫ], keep the front of your tongue against the alveolar ridge but try to say a long [uː]. You will feel the back of your tongue rising. Note that a great many words that end in dark [ɫ] have an [ʊ] sound immediately before (Mabel, unable, fatal).

PRACTICE

A.

(a) *clear* [l]

						[lj]
love	laugh	element	sleep	actually	English	failure
life	leg	eleven	slip	yellow	ticklish	million
look	Lord	alone	slope	silly	quickly	
lots	limp	along	sloppy	gorilla	lonely	

(b) *dark* [ɫ]

all	pool	curl	table	build	also
full	foal	snarl	marvel	field	wealthy
sell	growl	aisle	careful	gold	although

(c) *silent 'l'*

half	calm	talk	could	folk	colonel
calf	palm	chalk	should	yolk	salmon
halfpenny [heɪ́-]	almond	walk	would	Suffolk	

(d) As large as life.
Every cloud has a silver lining.
Let sleeping dogs lie.
Live and let live.
Love me little, love me long.
Little things please little minds.

B. (a) Do you really like living in a lighthouse all alone?
I absolutely love living in a lighthouse all alone.
(b) Do you lead a delightfully social life on Hollywood Boulevard?
Naturally, I lead . . .
(c) Have you ever lain in a sleeping bag on a lonely island in a total eclipse?
I've frequently lain . . .
(d) Does it look as if the long platform is actually parallel to the railway lines?
It certainly looks . . .

C. *Do you know where the stress comes in the names of these creatures?*

monkey	leopard	gorilla	lizard	hyena
giraffe	porcupine	spider	hippopotamus	squirrel
butterfly	donkey	kangaroo	elephant	peacock
crocodile	tiger	mosquito	tortoise	zebra
rhinoceros	nightingale	canary	chimpanzee	alligator

Answers: C.

mónkey	leópard	gorílla	lízard	hyéna
gíraffe	pórcupine	spíder	hippopótamus	squírrel
bútterfly	dónkey	kangaróo	élephant	péacock
crócodile	tíger	mosqúito	tórtoise	zébra
rhinóceros	níghtingale	canáry	chimpanzée	álligator

DIALOGUE 26. A lovely little lion

BILLY: I love wild life in its natural element. Look at all your lovely animals, Lucy. Lots and lots.
LUCY: Eleven, actually.
BILLY: And look! Here's a lovely little lion—a real live *black* lion asleep on the lawn.
LUCY: That's a leopard, actually.
BILLY: I don't believe it! Leopards are *yellow*. Look, Lucy, he's laughing! Do animals understand the English language?
LUCY: Leave him alone, Billy. He's licking his lips.
BILLY: Would you like a lettuce leaf, little lion?
LUCY: Billy, be careful—Oh Lord!
BILLY: Let go! Help, Lucy, he's got my leg!
LUCY: Actually, that's how I lost *my* left leg. You wouldn't listen, you silly fool. Well, let's limp over and look at the gorillas.

27. [r] run

Though in a number of languages [l] and [r] are not phonemic, in English they are, and it is important to distinguish clearly between them, both when listening and when speaking. When pronouncing [r] there is no gap on either side of the tongue. In fact, the tongue lies relaxed on the bottom of the mouth with only the tip raised towards the alveolar ridge. Now move the tip rapidly downwards so that it just brushes very briefly against the ridge and resumes its former position, at the same time expelling a little air and vibrating the vocal cords. This is a 'flapped' [r]. There is only one flap. Very often there is no flap at all ('fricative' [r]). The tongue lies still.
[r] is only pronounced before a vowel sound, not before a consonant nor at the end of a word: 'harm', 'bird', 'poor', 'there', 'later'.

PRACTICE

A.

(a)

roar	rare	rubbish	crying	carry	(w)rong
run	Rome	rabbit	drowning	worry	(w)rite
red	rage	river	Freddie	mirror	(w)rist
roof	rice	really	angry	tomorrow	(w)rap

silent 'r'

final position		*before consonant*		*before silent 'e'*		
car	poor	harm	fierce	there	pure	*N.B.* i(r)on
fur	later	bird	short	shore	fire	i(r)onmonger
near	prefer	turn	pearl	care	here	i(r)oning

(b) Round the rugged rock the ragged rascal rudely ran.
The hand that rocks the cradle rules the world.
Run rabbit, run rabbit, run, run, run.
Ring-a-ring o' roses.

Aurora Borealis.
Red as a beetroot.
Right as rain.
Merry Christmas, everybody!

B. *[r]/[l] contrast. Which is s/he saying?*

(a) I must remember to collect / correct the papers before tomorrow.

(b) Glamour / Grammar is all she lives for.

(c) The pilot / pirate signalled that he was coming alongside.

(d) I'm afraid I didn't bring the light / right suitcase.

(e) My lodger's / Roger's a solicitor.

C. *Here are a few minimal pairs with [l] and [r] for you to practise. There are lots and lots. How many can you think up?*

flog	bleed	belly	laughed	clash	alive
frog	breed	berry	raft	crash	arrive
long	fly	list	glow	glean	led
wrong	fry	wrist	grow	green	red

Answers: B. (a) collect (b) grammar (c) pirate (d) right (e) lodger's

DIALOGUE 27. The respective merits of frogs and rabbits

ROGER: My rabbit can roar like a rhinoceros.
BARRY: Rubbish! Rabbits don't roar, Roger.
ROGER: You're wrong, Barry. My rabbit's an Arabian rabbit. They're very rare. When he's angry he races round and round his rabbit run. And if he's in a real rage he rushes on to the roof and *roars*.
BARRY: How horrid! Really, I prefer my frog. I've christened him Fred.
ROGER: Freddie Frog! How ridiculous!
BARRY: An abbreviation for Frederick. Well, you remember when I rescued him from the river last February? He was crying like a canary. He was drowning.
ROGER: Really, Barry! Frogs don't drown.

28. Consonant sounds followed by [r]

Here we have some of the phonemes we have practised, followed immediately by [r]. Once you have mastered the individual sounds of these pairs, you should have no difficulty in pronouncing the two sounds together. Be careful not to roll your [r]—pronounce it nearer to [w] than [rrrr].
When the first sound is voiceless, as in [tr], [ʃr], [θr], etc., the air is expelled on the [r] and the following vowel, not on that first voiceless consonant itself.

PRACTICE

A.

(a)

cram	creek	crew	grove	thrift	crumble
gram	Greek	grew	drove	drift	grumble
tram	freak	true	shrove	shrift	
dram	shriek	through	trove		
pram	treacle	shrew	throve		

(b) *Work your way through the consonant sounds, putting [r] and the same vowel after each consonant (e.g. prat, brat, trat, drat, etc.) just for practice. You can look the words up in a dictionary to see if they actually exist!*

(c) *Some longer words*

miserable	unprofitable	untraceable	unanswerable
unfruitful	unshrinkable	unbreakable	immeasurable
incredible	undrinkable	ungrateful	unthreadable

B. (a) *Which is s/he saying?*

blessed	goes	cave	flows	cheese	Jack
breast	grows	crave	froze	trees	track
chain	quick	blink	junk	quest	jaw
drain	crick	brink	drunk	crest	draw

(b) *What are the missing words?*

1. Water is carried by the local . . .
2. There's too much . . . in the cities for my liking.
3. I'm afraid . . . is not my favourite food.
4. Only . . . men are allowed in the sanctuary.
5. Why don't we . . . the figs for a change?

C. *Mark the stressed syllables and underline the stronger stress in each word group.*

train crash	brick wall	train driver	huge great crate
dreadful dream	breathe properly	up front	pretty frightened
fresh fruit	incredibly brave	windscreen	broken crates

Answers: B. (a) breast grows cave froze cheese track
drain quick blink junk crest draw
(b) 1. train 2. grime 3. brawn 4. free 5. dry

C. train crash, dreadful dream, fresh fruit; brick wall, breathe properly, incredibly brave; train driver, up front, windscreen; huge great crate, pretty frightened, broken crates

DIALOGUE 28. A dreadful train crash

PRUE: Weren't you in that train crash on Friday, Fred?
FRED: Oh Prue, it's like a dreadful dream.
PRUE: A tractor—isn't that right?—crossing a bridge with a trailer of fresh fruit crashed through the brick wall in front of the train?
FRED: Yes. The train driver's a friend of my brother's. I was travelling up front with him. I was thrown through the windscreen on to the grass, but he was trapped under a huge great crate. I could hear him groaning.
PRUE: Fred! How grim!
FRED: I was pretty frightened, Prue, I can promise you! I crawled through the broken crates and tried to drag him free. His throat was crushed. He couldn't breathe properly, but he managed a grin.
PRUE: How incredibly brave!

29. Consonant clusters

Now we have groups of two, three and sometimes four consecutive consonant sounds with no vowel sound in between, e.g. [str], [ksp].
These 'consonant clusters', as they are called, are **not** difficult. Remember that in all languages the tendency is to pronounce things with the least amount of effort. So keep your lips and tongue and jaw as relaxed as possible—in some cases only the smallest movement is needed to slip from one sound to the next.
With words beginning with [s] + a consonant, be careful not to put an [e] sound before the [s]. Get the [s] right, hold on to it for a moment, then go on to the next sound.

PRACTICE

A.

extra extreme extr(a)ordin(a)ry	exchange expect explode	mixed taxed boxed	mixture fixture texture	picture adventure Christian
smashed crashed rushed	switched watched hatched	sergeant agent pageant	managed salvaged damaged	arranged exchanged singed
strawb(e)rry ras(p)b(e)rry blackb(e)rry	Pebble Beach probably veg(e)table	couldn't wouldn't oughtn't	acknowledge nickname bacon	Kingston amongst

B. *Listen to the dialogue. How many syllables are there in each of the following words?*

1. twenty-sixth
2. extremely
3. dangerous
4. extraordinarily
5. sergeant
6. strawberries
7. blackberry
8. headquarters
9. suspiciously
10. vegetables
11. emergency
12. transmitter
13. explosion
14. sufficient
15. shouldn't

C. *Mark the stressed syllables and then underline the strongest stress in each group of words.*

this extremely dangerous mission
an extraordinarily stupid sergeant
the village store

mashed potatoes
his emergency transmitter
a large blackberry and apple pie

Answers: B. 1. 3 2. 3 3. 3 4. 5 5. 2 6. 2 7. 2 8. 3
9. 4 10. 3 11. 4 12. 3 13. 3 14. 3 15. 2

C. this extrémely dángerous míssion
an extraórdinarily stúpid sérgeant
the víllage stóre

máshed potátoes
his emérgency transmítter
a lárge bláckberry and ápple píe

DIALOGUE 29: Two tricky problems

PARKER: There we were, the 26th Division, on this extremely dangerous mission, with only an extraordinarily stupid sergeant in charge.

MRS PARKER: If I managed to reach the village store before closing time, I wonder if Mrs Pecksmith would exchange the strawberries for a blackberry and apple pie . . . Just a sergeant, dear?

PARKER: The message came through from headquarters that we were to proceed to what we called Pebble Beach and examine a fishing boat that was behaving suspiciously.

MRS PARKER: That was a strange way for a fishing boat to behave . . . I could make the stuffed chicken stretch further with masses of mashed potatoes and fresh vegetables.

PARKER: The sergeant couldn't remember which switch to switch on his emergency transmitter. There we were, approaching the suspicious boat and suddenly there was an explosion like a . . . like a . . .

MRS PARKER: Like an earthquake, dear? . . . Then with a large blackberry and apple pie and whipped cream—there should be sufficient.

PARKER: Strictly speaking, the sergeant shouldn't have been in charge. I remember, the explosion split my trousers.

MRS PARKER: Well, go and change them, dear. The children will be here any minute.

30. Weak forms (1)

As we saw in Unit 13, to maintain the rhythm of speech in English, stressed syllables must be spoken at regular intervals of time and the unstressed syllables fitted into the gaps between the stresses. How is this possible if you're speaking at a reasonable speed? Well, we saw in Unit 12 that the vowels in unstressed syllables are often reduced to a rapid 'shwa' and sometimes even vanish altogether. In Unit 13 we looked briefly at groups of words that are not 'telegram words' and therefore usually have no stress. Here and in the next 2 units we shall consider these in more detail.
Note that the *normal* pronunciation is [ə] (the 'weak' form) and that the vowels in these words are only given their full value (the 'strong' form) if they are at the beginning or end of a sentence, or are being specially stressed (e.g. Are you coming, too? I hope you are. You *are* kind).

	A. *Weak forms (shwa)*	B. *Strong forms (full value)*
a, an [ə] [ən]	I swallowed a fly. An alligator bit him.	You say *a* book, *a* child, but *an* apple, *an* elephant.
am [əm] ['m]	What am I doing? I'm singing a song.	What *am* I to do? Am I serious? Yes, I'm afraid I am!
and [ən] ['n] [ənd]	Bread an(d) butter. Over an(d) over an(d) over again.	Trifle or jelly? Trifle *and* jelly, please! *And* she's a gossip . . .
are [ə] [ər]	Where are my glasses? Her cakes are awful!	They *are* mine, they *are*, they *are*! Are you alone?
as [əz]	I'm as happy as a king. Well, as far as I can see . . .	As I pour it on, you stir it. *As* I was saying before you interrupted.
at [ət]	I got it at a cheap shop. We're here at last!	He is selling it—but *at* a price. What are you staring at?
but [bət] [bə']	I'm ugly but intelligent! They say they are, but they're not.	'But me no "buts".' But for me, you would all be dead.
can [kən] [kn]	If you can do it, so can I. I can see a star.	Can I come too? Mother says I can.
could [kəd] [kd]	She said she could come. I'm so angry I could swear.	Could you possibly help me? There! I told you I could!
do [də] [d']	When do we begin? D'you understand?	Do look at that funny man! What do you do all day long?
does [dəz] [dz]	What time does it arrive? What does 2 and 2 make?	Does it work? Of course it does! Oh, she *does* look nice!

C. *Listen to the tape. The speakers are speaking very fast. What are they saying?*

Answers: C. I'm an expert at English but hopeless at French.
We're having meat and potatoes and a pudding.
Do you know, she ate a banana and an apple and a pear.
What do you want? What does anyone want?
I can sing as sweetly as a canary in a cage.
I'm pretending I'm an astronaut and you're an astronaut as well.

DIALOGUE 30. What a boring book you're reading!

JONATHAN: What are you doing, Elizabeth?
ELIZABETH: What am I doing? I'm reading. What does it look as though I'm doing?
JONATHAN: What are you reading?
ELIZABETH: A book, silly. What do you think? You can *see* I'm reading a book.
JONATHAN: I wish I could have a look at it. Do you think I could have a look at it, Elizabeth? Elizabeth, is it an interesting book?
ELIZABETH: Yes, a very interesting book. But an adult book. O.K., come and have a look at it and then go away and leave me alone.
JONATHAN: But what an awful book! It looks as boring as anything. How can you look at a book like that? What does it say?
ELIZABETH: Jonathan! *You're* an awfully boring and annoying little boy! Go away!

31. Weak forms (2)

Here is the second batch of words that are pronounced with a 'shwa' sound instead of having the full value of their vowels. Notice that on the whole these words are:

(i) articles (a, an, the),
(ii) personal pronouns (us, them, *etc.*),
(iii) prepositions (at, to, for, *etc.*),
(iv) auxiliary verbs (am, are, have, *etc.*),
(v) modal verbs (shall, should, must, can, *etc.*).

Notice also that in the case of some of them, particularly 'and' and 'must' and 'of', the final consonant is nearly always elided: 'and' is nearly always pronounced [ən]; 'must' and 'of' are usually pronounced [məs] and [ə] before a consonant.

When you're practising sentences or phrases, give the stresses exaggerated emphasis. This will make the unstressed words seem weak by comparison even if you're speaking fairly slowly and not weakening as much as a native speaker would. Keep the rhythm in mind all the time.

	A. *Weak forms (shwa)*	B. *Strong forms (full value)*
for [fə] [fr]	I'm doing it for fun. He's training for a race.	What did you do that for? For he's a jolly good fellow!
from [frəm] [frm]	They came from Africa. I'm speaking from experience.	I wonder where they came from? Guess where I got it from.
had [həd] [əd] [d]	You'd better put it back. Tell me, what had they done?	Had I finished this one last week? Yes, I think you had.
have [həv] [əv] [v]	We've put a frog in his bed! Why have you got a coat on?	Have you two met before? No, I don't think we have.
has [həz] [s] [z]	Charles has bought a car. What's he done now?	Has it stopped raining yet? He has got it, I know he has.
is [z] [s]	That's Concorde going over. She's a very good secretary.	Is this what you're looking for? She says she isn't, but she is.
must [məs] [məst]	I must go and buy a paper. Everyone must have a present.	Must you make so much noise? I must say, it's not bad!
not [nət] [nt]	I don't believe a word of it. They haven't finished yet.	Oh, not again! I told you not to! Raining? I hope not!
of [əv] [ə] [v]	I bought a pound of apples. Lots of people do it.	What's it all in aid of? Of the examples he gave, not one . . .
shall [ʃʊl] [ʃl] [l]	What shall we do if it rains? I'll tell your mother!	Shall I say you're out? If *you* don't, *I* shall!
should [ʃd]	You should look where you're going. I should think that's all right.	Should we call a doctor? I think we should.
some [səm] [sm]	They stole some money. We ate some chocolate.	Some people have all the luck! I made these myself. Do have some.

C. *Listen to the tape. What are the speakers saying?*

Answers: C. (a) I've had a letter from Jonathan. He doesn't say so but I'm afraid he isn't happy at school.
(b) I must go and make some sandwiches. The children are bringing some of their friends home for tea.
(c) I'll just go and see how Elizabeth's getting on. I should have gone yesterday. She's had 'flu, poor thing. I'll be as quick as I can. I'll be back before you've finished.

DIALOGUE 31. What have you done with Mabel?

SERENA: Barnabas, what have you done with that packet of biscuits?
BARNABAS: Well, there's a sort of an alligator in a cage over there. He looked sort of hungry.
SERENA: Barnabas, you didn't . . . ? But you must *never* feed an animal in a cage. I should think you've given it a bit of a stomach ache.
BARNABAS: He's been brought here from America.
SERENA: And anyway, I bought those biscuits for tea. What shall I tell Mother?
BARNABAS: I wish I'd got some cake for him as well, Serena. He's a nice alligator.
SERENA: But, my goodness, what have you done with little Mabel? Where's she gone?
BARNABAS: Well, she's . . . sort of . . . gone. He did look so sad so far from America, and *very* hungry.

32. Weak forms (3)

Here is the third and last group of words that have their normal pronunciation with a 'shwa' [ə] sound. Remember that the purpose of weakening the vowel sound is to make it possible for the word to be said more rapidly. Try to keep the unstressed syllables in each group exactly the same length as you speak, e.g.:

The one that was at the top
ðə / **wʌn** / ðə' / wəz / ə' / ðə / **tɒp**

(longer) (longest)
(louder) (loudest)
(higher) (highest)

Practise saying all the words with weakened vowels with the centre of your lips together, to prevent yourself from being led astray by the spelling. Listen to yourself and make sure that all the weakened vowel sounds are the same—ə, ən, əm, əz, ət, *etc*—and all of them 'shwa'!

	A. *Weak forms (shwa)*	B. *Strong forms (full value)*
than [ðən]	My sister's prettier than yours! It's easier than I expected.	*(not really possible)*
that [ðət] [ðə']	He said that I could have it. Tell her that I shan't be coming.	That's the man who shot him. That book belongs to me. I know that.
the [ðə]	The tiger ate the hunter. They dragged the body into the house.	Are yoú *the* William Shakespeare? My dear, they had the most awful row.
them [ðəm] [ðm]	Tell them I'm just coming. She gave them each a pound.	Don't give it to us, give it to them. 'Them as asks no questions, hears no lies!'
there [ðə] [ðər]	Is there a party tonight? There's a burglar in my bedroom!	Look, there he is, over there! There goes my last penny.
to [tə]	I went to London to see the Queen. I wanted to go to the cinema.	Who are you giving those flowers to? They got up to all kinds of mischief.
us [əs]	He told us to come back later. What do you want us to do?	So you told the Joneses, but not us! He's not going with you, he's coming with *us*.
was [wəz]	It was a dark and stormy night. I looked, but no one was there.	Was there any left in the bottle? I told you there was.
were [wə]	They were telling us about it. Hundreds of people were drowned.	Were you talking to me? I didn't know where you were.
would [wd] [wəd]	I'd like to have a word with you. Well, what would you have done?	Would you mind controlling your dog? Yes, I jolly well would!
you [jə]	Where are you going? What have you done with it?	You think you know everything. No one was talking to you.
your [jə]	Could you buy one on your way home? Don't put your hands in your pockets.	*Your* apples are rather small. I wouldn't like to be in your shoes!

DIALOGUE 32. There's nowhere to go in the jungle

CHRIS: Hi, Pete. All set for the final scene? Hey, what's the matter? You look as pale as a glass of vodka!

PETE: Barry and John have gone. Just upped and gone. While you were looking for the lake. I tried to stop them but there was nothing at all I could do—nothing that any of us could do.

CHRIS: What do you mean, gone? There's nowhere to go. In the middle of a Bolivian jungle? How would they get out?

PETE: They said there was a man who'd take them to the river—for an enormous fee—and that anything was better than dying of heat and mosquito bites in a South American jungle.

CHRIS: The miserable bastards! Well, go and get your camera, Pete. And the rest of the crew. We can survive without them. And I hope there's an alligator waiting for them at the river!

33. [ɪ] bit, bid

This is a very relaxed sound. The tongue lies with no tension on the bottom of the mouth, the lips are relaxed, slightly spread. It's probably best to close your mouth, make sure that there is no tension anywhere, then open your lips until you can just get one finger between them, open the teeth a *fraction* so that you can't get much more than a finger nail between them and then, without tensing up, say the sound you hear on the tape. To make doubly sure that you aren't tensing up at all, keep your fingers on your throat, just above your Adam's apple. Keep the vowel sound short.

PRACTICE

A.

(a)

big	dig	bin	din
pig	rig	pin	sin
fig	wig	thin	win

You can go through all the consonant sounds just to practise. It doesn't matter if you're not making actual words.

(b)

primitive	thick-skinned	six sinking ships
ministry	twin sisters	Isn't it a little bit thin?
antiquity	stinking rich	a picnic in the hills
distinguishing	unsolicited gift	the Sicilian Fishing Industry
Mississippi	British history	fish and chips

(c) There's many a slip 'twixt the cup and the lip.
If the cap fits, wear it.
As fit as a fiddle.
As pretty as a picture.
Little pitchers have big ears.

B. *Some deceptive spellings*

misses	watches	wanted	added	sacred	aged
freezes	fixes	fitted	faded	crooked	learned
washes	wages	waited	weeded	wicked	beloved
believe	kitchen	poet	silliness	mischief	anemone
before	women	perfect	mattress	handkerchief	recipe
refuse	English	earnest	limitless	sieve	catastrophe
private	privacy	cottage	cabbage	college	passenger
fortunate	palace	village	damage	privilege	messenger
deliberate	purchase	marriage	courage		orange
busy	biscuit	hymn	Monday	vineyard	pretty
minute	building	idyllic	birthday	sovereign	
lettuce	circuit	physics	holiday		

C. *Here are some British place names that contain the [ɪ] sound. Some are fairly straightforward, but some of them are deceptive. You will have to listen carefully.*

Hitchen	Denbigh	Hadleigh	Wensleydale
Chiswick	Uist	Bicester	King's Lynn
Ipswich	Salisbury	Gullane	Inverbervie
Edinburgh	Bideford	Chipstead	Manchester
Lewes	Dorset	Plymouth	Kirkcudbright
Lincoln	Swansea	Inverary	Merthyr Tydfil

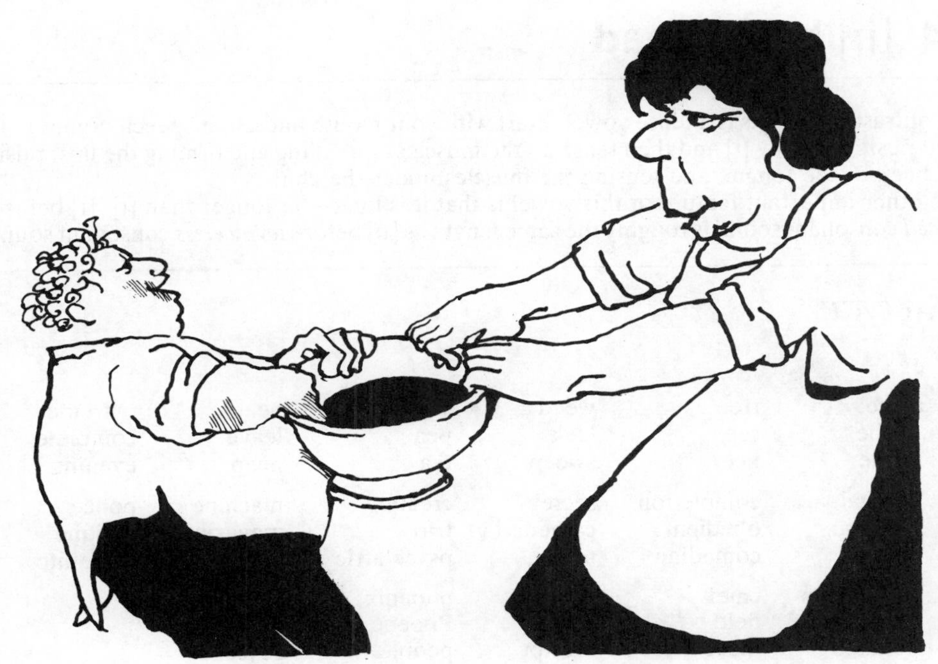

DIALOGUE 33. Busy in the kitchen

BILLY: Mummy! Are you busy?
MOTHER: Yes. I'm in the kitchen.
BILLY: Can I go swimming in Chichester with Jim this morning?
MOTHER: Jim?
BILLY: Jim English. He's living with Mr and Mrs Willis in the village—Spring Cottage.
MOTHER: Isn't it a bit chilly to go swimming?
BILLY: What's this? Can I pinch a bit of it?
MOTHER: Oh, Billy, you little pig! It's figgy pudding. Get your fingers out of it!
BILLY: Women are so silly! I only dipped a little finger in.
MOTHER: Well, it's a filthy little finger. Here, tip this chicken skin into the bin and I'll give you a biscuit.

34. [iː] beat, bead

In contrast to [ɪ], this is a tense vowel. Start with your mouth and other speech organs in the right position to say [ɪ] and then tense all the muscles, spreading and firming the lips, raising the back of the tongue and tensing the muscles under the chin.
The other important feature of this vowel is that it is long—far longer than [ɪ]. [ɪ] before a *voiced* consonant sound is roughly the same length as [iː] before a *voiceless* consonant sound.

PRACTICE

A.

(a)

he	tree	weed	sea	beans	extreme
she	see	leek	pea	leave	complete
me	flee	sweep	tea	heap	evening
legal	completion	secret	create	machine	police
equal	obedient	cathedral	trio	magazine	antique
evil	comedian	metre	psychiatric	sardine	mosquito
Achilles	chief	deceive	phoenix	key	
Ulysses	field	ceiling	Phoebe	quay	
crises	niece	receipt	people	geyser	
Aesop	Caesar	Leigh	Beauchamp		

(b) *'the' before a vowel*—the animal, the end, the answer
words ending in '-y' before a vowel—a lovely antique, you silly idiot!

(c) *short and long*

beat:bead	seat:sea
leaf:leaves	teach:tea
wheat:weed	feet:fee

(d) *N.B. No difference in pronunciation between:*

key—quay	seize—seas
beet—beat	week—weak
see—sea	ceiling—sealing

(e) *minimal pairs*

bit	hill	hip	still	fit	sit	grin	sin
beat	heel	heap	steel	feet	seat	green	seen

(f) It's all Greek to me.
A friend in need is a friend indeed.
New brooms sweep clean.
Easy come, easy go.

B. *Which is s/he saying?*

(a) Shall we slip / sleep in here?

(b) We had a wonderful mill / meal by the river.

(c) I've never seen a ship / sheep move so fast!

(d) We're going to live / leave here very soon.

(e) Don't tell me you bit / beat your brother!

Answers: B. (a) slip (b) meal (c) sheep (d) live (e) beat

DIALOGUE 34. Weeding's not for me!

PETER: This is the season for weeds. We'll each weed three metres before tea, easily.
CELIA: Do we kneel? My knees are weak. Do you mean all these?
PETER: Celia, my sweet, those aren't weeds, those are seedlings. Beans, peas and leeks. Can't you *see*?
CELIA: If they're green they're weeds to me. But I agree, Peter—weeding's not for me!
PETER: Well, let me see. May be we'll leave the weeds. You see these leaves? If you sweep them into a heap under that tree I'll see to the tea.
CELIA: Pete, my feet are freezing. *You* sweep the leaves. I'll see to the tea!

35. [e] bet, bed

This is a relaxed sound, like [ɪ]. The mouth is just a little more open than for [ɪ]; you should be able to put a finger between your teeth, and the lips are a little wider apart than that. Keep the sound short. And be careful not to open your mouth too much or you will find that you are saying the next sound [æ].

PRACTICE

A.

(a)

Ken	bend	west	seven	direction	head
ten	send	chest	clever	reckon	heavy
when	mend	dressed	never	adventure	treasure
very	medal	berry	heather	leisure	said
merit	petal	terror	weather	Leicester	again *also* [əgeɪn]
heron	lemon	errand	death	Reynolds	against
says	any	leopard	friend	haemorrhage	bury
ate	many	Leonard	friendly		
Thames		Geoffrey			

(b) Least said, soonest mended.
All's well that ends well.
Rain before seven, fine before eleven.
Better late than never.
The thin end of the wedge.
Marry in haste, repent at leisure.
There's a remedy to everything but death.
God defend me from my friends; from my enemies I can defend myself.
Every day and in every way, I get better and better and better.

B.

Which is s/he saying?

(a) Orpheus went down to Hell. / the hill.

(b) Did you get back the pen / pin you lent him?

(c) Did you finish the hem / hymn then?

(d) I said I felt the bed / bid was too high.

(e) He put everything in his well. / will.

(f) Many were / Minnie was rescued but Minnie / many perished.

(g) What did Belle / Bill tell Bill? / Belle?

C. *Listen to the dialogue. Mark the stressed syllables.*

heaven	desperate	direction	bury
treasure	remember	sunset	yesterday
eleven	reckon	adventure	again

Answers: B. (a) to Hell (b) pen (c) hymn (d) bed (e) will (f) Minnie, many (g) Belle, Bill
C. héaven tréasure eléven désperate remémber réckon diréction súnset advénture búry yésterday agáin

DIALOGUE 35. The end of the adventure

KEN: Ted! Thank heaven! I was getting desperate.
TED: Hello there, Ken. Where are Jeff and the rest of the men?
KEN: They left me in the tent with some eggs and some bread, and off they went.
TED: Where were they heading?
KEN: West. In that direction. They said they'd bury the treasure under the dead elm—you remember, by the bend in the fence—and get back by sunset.
TED: All ten of them went?
KEN: They said the chest was heavy.
TED: They left—when?
KEN: Yesterday, between ten and eleven.
TED: And you *let* them?
KEN: There were *ten* of *them* . . .
TED: Well, my friend, I reckon that's the end of the adventure. We'll never see the treasure chest or any of those ten men again.

36. [æ] bat, bad

This is another short vowel, but the mouth is wider open than for [e]. Press the tip of your tongue hard against your lower teeth, bunch the tongue up behind it, open your lips so that the corners of your mouth are not pressed together, and then make a bleating sound, like a lamb. The sound you are trying to achieve is very like that which a lamb makes, but perhaps it would be wise to practise in private to begin with!

PRACTICE

A.

(a)

Jack	gang	cash	ham	man	grand
crackle	sang	crash	jam	Gran	sandwich
racket	sprang	splash	Sam	fantastic	understand

				short and long vowels
apple	album	clarity	static	mat:mad
cattle	animal	charity	ecstatic	back:bag
handle	asthma	personality	dramatic	catch:cadge

Spanish	palace	granite	acid	cabin	examine
radish	Alice	Janet	rapid	Latin	imagine
Adam	camel	travel	cavern	balance	shadow
madam	enamel	gravel	tavern	salad	gather

(b)

girls' names			*boys' names*		
Janet	Ann	Sally	Jack	Daniel	Nathaniel
Marion	Annabel	Hanna	Harry	Anthony	Basil
Miranda	Caroline	Joanna	Alec	Sam	Alan

(c) Flat as a pancake.
A matter of fact.
Mad as a hatter.

Catch as catch can.
A hungry man is an angry man.
May as well be hanged for a sheep as a lamb.

B. *Which is s/he saying?*

(a) I said he could go to Hal / Hell.

(b) Look at that fabulous jam. / gem.

(c) When did Adam tell you he'd sand / send the paving stones?

(d) Did you remember to bring back the cattle? / kettle?

(e) There are too many gnats / nets about.

C. *Listen to the dialogue. Mark the stressed syllables.*

piano	album	fantastic	absolute	talent	understand
practising	racket	galactic	Grandad	sandwich	static

Answers: B. (a) Hell (b) jam (c) send (d) cattle (e) gnats
C. piano, practising, album, racket, fantastic, galactic, absolute, Grandad, talent, sandwich, understand, static

DIALOGUE 36. Crackle, crackle, Galactic Static

GRAN: Jack, do you have to bang and slam on that piano like that?
JACK: I'm practising for our new album. It's smashing.
GRAN: An album? You mean that racket you and your gang bash out?
JACK: We're not a gang, we're a fantastic jazz band. Sally and Janet, me on the piano, Alec on the sax—the Galactic Static. It'll be an absolute smash hit.
GRAN: The Galactic Racket, if you ask me. And all you'll smash is Grandad's piano.
JACK: Gran, we have *talent*. We're cool cats, man. Crackle, crackle, Galactic Static!
GRAN: The young man's mad. Here. I've made you a fat ham sandwich and a crab-apple jam flan.
JACK: Ah, Gran, you may not understand jazz but your flans are fab.

37. [ʌ] cut, come

This is a relaxed, short sound. The lips and teeth are a **little** more open than for [e]—which, if you remember, was slightly more open than for [ɪ]. Get your mouth and tongue ready to say [ɪ] (*hit*, *him*, *hip*), nicely relaxed. Now open your mouth till you can just slip the tips of two half-crossed fingers between your teeth. The bottom finger should be able to feel the tip of your tongue still lying relaxed behind your bottom teeth.

Don't draw back your lips or tense your muscles—you will be saying [æ] again. And don't raise the back of your tongue too much or you will be saying sound No. 38, [ɑː]. Keep the sound short.

PRACTICE

A.

(a)

fun	cut	luck	jump	rug	crum(b)
sun	shut	duck	trust	swum	thum(b)
begun	butter	stuck	shut	stung	dum(b)

(b) *In each of these words, the stressed syllable contains the sound [ʌ] even though you may not think so from the spelling.*

son	one	onion	London	among	constable
ton	done	honey	Monday	tongue	front
won	once	money	wonder	mongrel	sponge
come	comfort	above	shovel	govern	
some	company	dove	cover	oven	
stomach	compass	glove	discover	slovenly	
other	nothing	double	rough		
mother	thorough	couple	tough		
brother	month	country	enough		
blood	does	cousin	touch	twopence	worry
flood	doesn't	dozen	young	colour	wonder

(c) Lucky in cards, unlucky in love.
What's done cannot be undone.

Not in a month of Sundays.
Well begun is half done.

The rain it raineth on the just and unjust fella,
But more upon the just, because the unjust's got the just's umbrella.

B. *Listen to the tape and fill in the missing words*

'. . . . , ... Are you . . . . to . . . . on . . . . ? . . . . and have . . . . at my . . . . .' '. . . . to. I've been . . . . in the . . . . for . . . . .'
'I was . . . .—. . . .what had . . . . of you.'
'. . . . a . . . . of . . . . A bit . . . . I shall . . . . .'
'. . . . . I . . . . , ... See you at the . . . . on . . . . at . . . . .'
'. . . . . My . . . . to your . . . . .'

Answers: B. 'Hullo, Uncle Duncan. Are you coming up to London on Monday? Come and have lunch at my Club.'
'Love to. I've been stuck in the country for months.'
'I was worried—wondered what had become of you.'
'Just a touch of lumbago. Nothing much. A bit troublesome sometimes. Uncomfortable. I shall recover.'
'Tough luck. I must run, Uncle. See you at the Club on Monday at one.'
'Wonderful. My love to your mother.'

DIALOGUE 37. The bungalow's flooded

DUNCAN: Jump up, Cuthbert! The bungalow's flooded!

CUTHBERT: The bungalow? Flooded?

DUNCAN: Come on, hurry up.

CUTHBERT: Just our luck! We're comfortably in London for a month, come down to the country on Sunday—and on Monday we're flooded! Trust us!

DUNCAN: Shut up! Come on, double up the rugs and stuff them above the cupboard. Chuck me that shovel. There's a ton of rubble that I dug out of the rubbish dump. I'll shove it under the front door—it seems to be coming from the front.

CUTHBERT: Duncan! I'm stuck!

DUNCAN: Oh, brother! You're as much use as a bloody duck!

CUTHBERT: If I'd been a duck, I could have swum! Oh crumbs! The mud's coming in under the other one! We're done for! We'll be sucked into the disgusting stuff!

DUNCAN: Hush! How wonderful! The current's suddenly swung. It's not going to touch us . . . unless . . . I wonder . . .

38. The Tonic

In previous units we have looked at stress within words, in noun–adjective groups and in compound nouns. The *main* stress *usually* comes on the last stressed word of a sentence. Now we shall see how you can alter the whole meaning of a sentence simply by shifting the point of main stress—the TONIC, as it is called.

In the sentence 'John didn't speak to Mavis', the main stress will normally be on '*Mavis*', holding the listener's attention right to the end of the sentence. But if you alter the stress you can imply all sorts of different things:

John didn't speak to Mavis (Peter did)
John *didn't* speak to Mavis (you've got it all wrong)
John didn't *speak* to Mavis (he *wrote* to her)

or exaggerated stress on Mavis:

John didn't speak to *Mavis* (he spoke to Anna).

Notice how after the Tonic, what's left of the sentence stays at the same pitch, with very little stress even on normally stressed syllables.

PRACTICE

A. *Listen to the tape. Where is the Tonic in these sentences?*

(a) We didn't mean to arrive just in time for lunch.
(b) Is this the book you were looking for?
(c) But you told me I could come round tonight.
(d) I haven't seen Elizabeth for ages.
(e) No, dear. He broke his leg in a skiing accident.
(f) Are all nine of the Joneses coming to dinner?

B. *Now practise shifting the Tonic yourself:*

(a) Are you coming to Majorca with us this *summer*?
Are you coming to Majorca with us *this* summer?
Are you coming to Majorca with *us* this summer?
Are you coming to *Majorca* with us this summer?
Are *you* coming to Majorca with us this summer?
Are you coming to Majorca with us this summer?

(b) *My* wife doesn't look like a sack of potatoes.
My *wife* doesn't look like a sack of potatoes.
My wife *doesn't* look like a sack of potatoes.
My wife doesn't *look* like a sack of potatoes.
My wife doesn't look like a *sack* of potatoes.
My wife doesn't look like a sack of *potatoes*.

C. *Can you add something to each sentence to explain the implication of the change of stress in the sentences in Question B?*

Answers: A. (a) mean (b) this (c) told (d) ages (e) skiing (f) nine

B. (suggestions only)

(a) – even if you can't come in the spring.
– since you didn't come *last* summer.
– or are you going with the Joneses?
– or are you going to Cyprus?
– or is it only your parents who are coming?
– For goodness' sake, make up your mind!

(b) – thank goodness! But *your* wife does.
– but my mother-in-law does.
– It's not true! She's beautiful!
– though I admit she feels like one.
– she looks like a whole lorry load of them!
– she looks like a sack of cabbages.

DIALOGUE 38. I've won a prize!

MICHAEL: Jennifer! Guess what! I've won a prize!

JENNIFER: A prize? What sort of prize?

MICHAEL: A super prize. Dinner for two at Maxime's!

JENNIFER: You are clever! What was the prize for? I mean, what did you do to win a dinner for two at Maxime's?

MICHAEL: Well, you're not to laugh—I went in for a competition at the Adult Education Centre—a cooking contest.

JENNIFER: You won a prize in a cooking contest! I've got to laugh. Michael, you can't even boil an egg!

MICHAEL: I can boil an egg. I can scramble one, too. Most deliciously. Of course, I'm not a Cordon Bleu cook, like you . . .

JENNIFER: Well, why haven't I ever won a cooking competition?

MICHAEL: Probably because you never go in for competitions. I'm glad you didn't go in for this one. You might have won, and then you would have had to invite me to dinner at Maxime's!

39. [ɒ] boss, bomb

This is another short sound. But this time it is tense. The teeth should be about the width of a thumb apart, with the lips pushed forward and held stiffly about the same distance apart as the teeth. The back of the tongue is drawn right up towards the roof of the mouth and the tip of the tongue lies on the bottom of the mouth as far back as it will go. Imagine that you have a very hot potato in your mouth, just behind your bottom teeth!

PRACTICE

A.

(a)

chop	box	cost	song	off	toffee
flop	crocks	frost	wrong	cough	robber
stop	knocks	hostel	belong	trough	copper
bottle	doctor	body	model	what	because
topple	blonde	promise	proper	squat	sausage
jostle	problem	holiday	Roger	swat	cauliflower
cloth	knowledge	Jorrocks	quantity	Australia	
bother	acknowledge	jollity	quality	Austria	

(b) Honesty is the best policy.
A watched pot never boils.
When sorrow is asleep, wake it not.

'Once upon a time there were three little foxes
Who didn't wear stockings, and they didn't wear sockses . . .
But they all had handkerchiefs to blow their noses,
And they kept their handkerchiefs in cardboard boxes.'

B. *Try to say these with a regular rhythm, like a chant:*

What we want is Watneys.
What we want is Top of the Pops.
What we want is to stop the rot.
What we want is a holiday in Scotland.
What we want's a proper copper on the job.

C. *Listen to the tape. Which word in each of these place names has the main stress?*

Onslow Square
Cromarty Gardens
Hot Cross Lane
Bosworth Terrace

Notting Hill Gate
Connemara Crescent
Horse Trough Road
Cauliflower Green

Sollihul Circus
Gossip's Row
Pocklington Place
Oxford Street

Answers: C. They all have major stress on the last word, *except* the final one. In the name of a *street* the name itself has the main stress.

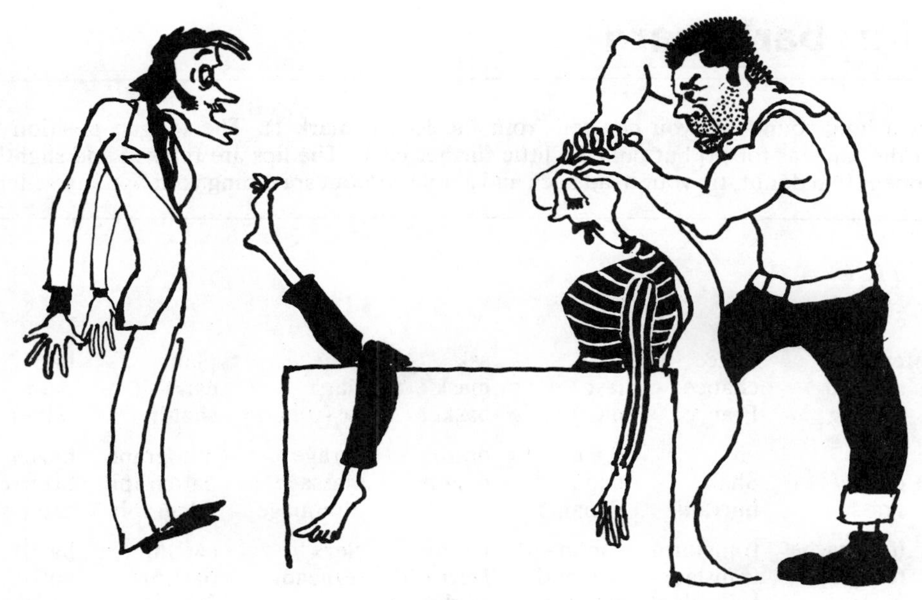

DIALOGUE 39. What's wrong with the blonde popsy?

BOB: Sorry, Tom. I wasn't gone long, was I? My God! What's wrong with the blonde popsy? She looks odd—sort of floppy.

TOM: No longer a blonde popsy, old cock—a body.

BOB: Oh my God! You gone off your rocker? I just pop off to the shop for a spot of . . .

TOM: Stop your slobbering, you clot! So we got a spot of bother. Come on, we got to squash the blonde into this box and then I want lots of cloths and a pot of water—hot—and probably a mop—to wash off all these spots.

BOB: Clobbering a blonde! It's not on, Tom!

TOM: Put a sock in it, Bob, or I'll knock your block off!
(*Knock, knock.*)

BOB: Oh my God! What's that knocking? Tom, Tom, it's a copper!

40. [ɑː] bark, barn

This is a long sound (as you can tell from the length mark ː). The tongue position is almost the same as for [ʌ] but pulled a little further back. The lips are relaxed and slightly more open. If in doubt, tip your head back and gargle without spreading your lips any wider.

PRACTICE

A.

(a)

car	dance	past	ask	gasp	plant	bath
starved	chance	last	mask	clasp	can't	path
darling	France	nasty	basket	ras(p)berry	shan't	father
pass	ah	mama	drama	garage	autograph	bazaar
class	Shah	papa	pyjama	massage	paragraph	bizarre
grass	hurrah!	Panama	banana	espionage	telegraph	catarrh
moustache	transform	command	Derby	clerk	ca(l)m	ha(l)f
tomato	translate	demand	Hertford	sergeant	pa(l)m	ha(l)ves
Yugoslavia	transplant	slander	Berkshire		(p)salm	ca(l)f
					a(l)mond	ca(l)ves
example	staff	branch	laughed	heart	aunt	after
sample	giraffe	avalanche	draught	hearth	aren't	answer

(b)

Marble Arch	a hard bargain	Charlie is my darling
draught lager	a heart transplant	a clerk in Berkeley Castle
half mast	the Star and Garter	from Derby to Clerkenwell

(c) He who laughs last laughs longest.
One is nearer God's heart in a garden.
Cold hands, warm heart.
Part and parcel.

B. *[ɒ] is always shorter than [ɑː] even when [ɑː] is followed by a voiceless consonant sound. Try saying these words, first in columns, keeping the words in the first column really short, in the second a little bit longer and so on. Then read them across, increasing the length of the vowel as you move from left to right.*

hot	hod	heart	hard
cot	cod	cart	card
pot	pod	part	pard
lock	log	lark	Largs
off	of	half	halves

C. *Listen to the dialogue and mark the stressed syllables, then underline the Tonic in each group of words.*

(a) Ah, here we are.
(b) Your father's car's draughty.
(c) Your moustache is all nasty and sharp.
(d) It's only Sergeant Barker.
(e) You can't start making a pass till after the dance.

Answers: C. (a) Ah, here we are. (b) Your father's car's draughty. (c) Your moustache is all nasty and sharp. (d) It's only Sergeant Barker. (e) You can't start making a pass till after the dance.

DIALOGUE 40. Making a pass at Martha

CHARLIE: The dance doesn't start till half past, Martha. Let's park the car under the arch by Farmer Palmer's barn. It's not far. Ah, here we are. There's the farm cart.

MARTHA: Ooh, Charlie, it's dark!

CHARLIE: The stars are sparkling. My heart is enchanted. Martha you are—marvellous!

MARTHA: Your father's car's draughty, Charlie. Pass me my scarf.

CHARLIE: Rather let me clasp you in my arms, Martha, my darling.

MARTHA: Ah, Charlie! Your moustache is all nasty and sharp. I can't help laughing. Aren't you starved? Here, have half a Mars Bar. Ssh! There's a car passing.

CHARLIE: Keep calm, can't you? It's only Sergeant Barker. He plays darts in the bar of the Star and Garter. Martha . . . darling . . .

MARTHA: Don't be daft, Charlie! You can't start making a pass till after the dance!

41. [ɔː] bought, board

Another long sound, and an easy one to move on to once you have mastered [ɑː]. Say [ɑː], then, keeping your tongue and teeth absolutely rigid, move your lips together and forward so that they form an 'O' about the same distance apart as your teeth. Did you keep these, and your tongue, just as they were for [ɑː]? If you hold your thumb sideways and then bite it, the inside of your lips should just touch it. If you're making too small an 'O', you'll find that you're saying [uː]. Like [ɑː], [ɔː] comes from very far back, almost in the nasal passage.

PRACTICE

A.

(a)

or	more	storm	oral	four
for	store	corn	glory	your
nor	before	tortoise	chorus	course
poor	boar	ought	all	bald
door	roar	thought	call	salt
floor	soar	bought	stall	Malta
awe	lawn	autumn	toward	taught
jaw	crawl	August	reward	caught
thaw	awful	aural	warder	daughter
hoarse	board	cha(l)k	sta(l)k	sward
coarse	hoard	ta(l)k	wa(l)k	s(w)ord
water	Montreal	shore	altar	poor
launder	Nepal	sure	alter	pour

Paul – Pauline   George – Georgina   Norman – Norma

(b) Any port in a storm.
The calm before the storm.
New Lords, new laws.
Pride comes before a fall.
To put the cart before the horse.
A tall order.
You can take a horse to the water, but you can't make it drink.

B. *Which is s/he saying?*

(a) This collar / colour won't stay on properly.

(b) What a horrible shock! / shark!

(c) I think he's been shot / shut in the chest.

(d) What have you done with the cups? / corpse?

(e) You played the wrong chord / card just then.

(f) What's that filthy mark / muck on your jeans?

(g) I cooked the pears in father's port. / pot.

Answers: B. (a) collar (b) shark (c) shot (d) corpse (e) card (f) muck (g) port

DIALOGUE 41. Fawns, horses and a tortoise

PAUL: Any more of these awful autumn storms, George, and we'll be short of corn. I ought to have bought some more in Northport.

GEORGE: This morning, just before dawn, I thought I saw signs of a thaw. I was sure—

PAUL: Ssh! Behind that door there are four fawns that were born in the storm. They're all warm in the straw now.

GEORGE: Poor little fawns! Paul, what's that snorting next door?

PAUL: Those are the horses' stalls. They're snorting at my daughter's tortoise. It always crawls around in the straw.

GEORGE: If Claud saw us walking across his lawn . . . He's an awful bore about his lawn. Oh, Lord, we're caught! There *is* Claud! Now we're for it!

42. Elision

Rhythm, it cannot be emphasised enough, is all important. In order to keep the rhythm flowing, consonant sounds are sometimes dropped altogether; for instance, in words like cu(p)board, ras(p)berry, gran(d)mother, han(d)kerchief. This is known as ELISION.

When the same sound occurs at the end of one word and at the beginning of the next, they are not produced as two separate sounds, but held on to without a break for a little longer than a single sound. In the English phrases 'Don't talk', 'I want to', the first [t] is not aspirated at all. Your speech organs are all in the correct position but you don't let go of the sound until the rhythm dictates that it is time to start the second word.

When one of the first six sounds we looked at (the 'plosives') occurs at the end of a word, with a different consonant sound at the beginning of the next word ('good thing', 'take time'), your speech organs prepare to say the first sound, hesitate on it, and then move on to the second consonant sound. This blocking of the first sound is known as a 'Glottal Stop'.

If this first consonant sound is suppressed, how can one know what it was meant to be? The answer is that something of the sound you were preparing to say attaches itself to the sound you *do* say; and the context and the meaning of the sentence as a whole help the listener to understand; and the length of the preceding vowel indicates whether the suppressed consonant was voiced or voiceless. The only way we can really tell the difference between 'Batman' and 'bad man' is that in the first, the first syllable is short, in the second, long. Some sounds such as [s] and [h] are so easy to slide on to after a plosive that you simply run them together as if the second sound were part of the aspiration of the first.

PRACTICE

A. (a) *Same consonant sound*

good‿dog	don't‿talk	Arab‿boy	cough‿first
stop‿pushing	well‿left	jam‿making	the fourth‿Thursday
ask‿Kate	those‿zoos	Italian‿navy	with‿this
this‿sausage	big‿game	I love‿Venice	low‿water

[tʃ] and [dʒ] are two-sound combinations. Both sounds have to be repeated [tʃ-tʃ], [dʒ-dʒ]).

Dutch cheese	Judge Jones	a rich journalist
fetch Charles	large gin	the village champion

(b) *Plosive followed by a different consonant*

lo(g) cabin	nigh(t) boat	sudde(n) glimpse	u(p) north
straigh(t) road	thic(k) dark	re(d) log	aprico(t)-coloured
Arcti(c) trip	dee(p) moss	brillian(t) yellow	ta(k)e pictures

B. *Which is s/he saying?*

(a) We step / stepped down.
(b) I like / liked Don.
(c) We went for a long / longer walk.
(d) I look / I'll look carefully.
(e) It's a nice / nicer song.
(f) I always kick / kicked Kate.

C. *Changing the position of the stress in a word can alter its meaning or its function. There is a whole group of two-syllable words that have the stress on the first syllable when a word is being used as a noun, and on the second when it's a verb,*

e.g. progress n. Now you are making good prógress.
v. You will never progréss until you learn to listen.
export n. Are all your goods for éxport?
v. Nearly all. We expórt 90% of our total production.

Now you try changing the stress on the following words, making up sentences if you can:

import	record	contract	object	permit	convert
present	produce	desert	insult	protest	transport

Answers: B. (a) stepped (b) like (c) long (d) I'll look (e) nicer (f) kicked

DIALOGUE 42. A trip to Lapland

TOM: Well, Louise! I was just talking about you! When did you get back from your Arctic trip?

LOUISE: Last night, Tom, about twelve. We caught the night boat from Malmö. Jos said it was a bit late to telephone neighbours.

TOM: Did you have a good time? What's Lapland like? I've never been there.

LOUISE: It's just beautiful, Tom, I can't tell you. Great rocks of pink granite. Thick dark forests carpeted with deep moss and wild strawberries and lily of the valley. Sudden glimpses of red log cabins and bright blue water. Fields of brilliant yellow.

TOM: I thought Lapland would be quite different—wilder, more rugged? And is it true, all that talk of the Midnight Sun?

LOUISE: Right up north, yes. I couldn't get used to the light nights at first. But, Tom, magic isn't the word! That glowing apricot-coloured sky. And the marvellous silence—absolute peace.

TOM: What about the mosquitoes? I've been told they can be quite nasty.

LOUISE: Ugh! Great big fat things! Every time we stopped to take pictures or pick cloudberries, we were just devoured.

43. [uː] loose, lose

This is a long sound (as you can see from the mark ː). The tongue is in the same position as for [ɑː] and [ɔː] but the lips are tightly pursed. Say [ɑː] to make sure of the tongue position. Then stop the sound, but without moving the tongue close your teeth almost completely, push your lips right forward and together into a tight little bud. Open them just enough to close fairly tightly round one finger, and vibrate your vocal cords.

PRACTICE

A.

(a)

loo	shoot	food	proof	do	who
tool	boot	spoon	tooth	too	whom
fool	root	school	Hoover	two	whose
soup	tomb	move	loose	shoe	screw
group	womb	prove	lose	canoe	blew
through	catacomb	movie			chew
June	Sue	ruling	conclusion	Rufus	truth
rude	blue	Lucy	Peruvian	prudent	Ruth
super	true	lucid	crucial	lunatic	sleuth
[uː]			[uːɪ]		
suit	juice	bruise	ruin	druid	suicide
fruit	sluice	cruise	Bruin	fluid	Suez
[juː]					
Hugh	fuse	Kew	tulip	human	future
huge	amuse	few	tutor	usual	music
tune	abuse	new	student	useful	museum
costume	you	cue	adieu	queue	beauty
vacuum	youth	value	neuter		
monument		argue	Euston		
[juːɪ]					
Buick	reviewing	queuing	genuine	tuition	

(b) Beauty is truth, truth beauty.
The proof of the pudding is in the eating.
Music hath charms to soothe the savage breast.
Fortune favours fools.
An eye for an eye and a tooth for a tooth.

B. *Where is the stress in the names of these wild birds?*

woodpecker	swallow	ostrich	robin
kingfisher	sparrow	blackbird	magpie
eagle	pigeon	wagtail	skylark
parrot	starling	partridge	goldfinch
pheasant	heron	nightingale	cormorant

Answers: B. Easy, wasn't it? The stress is on the first syllable in all of them.

DIALOGUE 43. Where are you, Hugh?

LUCY: Hugh? Yoo hoo! Hugh! Where are you?
HUGH: I'm in the loo. Where are *you*?
LUCY: Removing my boots. I've got news for you.
HUGH: News? Amusing news?
LUCY: Well, I saw June in Kew. You know how moody and rude she is as a rule? Hugh, are you *still* in the loo? What are you *doing*?
HUGH: Well, you see, Lucy, I was using the new foolproof screwdriver on the Hoover and it blew a fuse.
LUCY: You fool! I knew that if I left it to you, you'd do something stupid. You usually do.
HUGH: And then I dropped the screwdriver down the loo.
LUCY: Hugh, look at your shoes! And your new blue suit! It's ruined! And you—you're wet through!
HUGH: To tell you the truth, Lucy—I fell into the loo, too.

44. [ʊ] foot, good

This is a short vowel sound and, unlike 43, the muscles are relaxed. Say the sound [uː] and then relax the top lip and the tongue slightly. There is still a little tension in the muscles and the lips are still slightly pursed. Don't relax too much and don't let your jaw drop or you will find that you are pronouncing 'shwa' [ə] instead.

PRACTICE

A.

(a)

wood	book	bull	bush	sugar
good	look	bully	cushion	pudding
stood	took	bullet	butcher	cuckoo
could	wolf	table	miserable	apple
would	wolves	cradle	sensible	middle
should	Wolsey	Naples	syllable	uncle
usual	special	faculty	backwards	Worcester
casual	partial	difficult	forwards	worsted
		[jʊ]		
foot	wool	cure	furious	maturity
soot	woollen	pure	curious	endurance
put	gooseberry	woman	bosom	Michael

(b) *The weak form of 'shall' and 'will'*

Bill'll be furious. What shall we do?
I shall tell the curate. Tony'll cook the dinner.

B. (a) Could you cook a gooseberry pudding without putting sugar in?
No, I couldn't cook a gooseberry pudding without putting sugar in.
(b) Could you pull a camel who was miserable, looked awful and said he didn't want to travel, all the way from Fulham to Naples?
No, I couldn't pull . . .
(c) Could you walk through a wood, knowing it was full of horrible wolves, and not pull your hood up and wish you didn't look edible?
No, I couldn't walk . . .

C. *[uː]/[ʊ] contrast. Which word in each pair is said twice?*

fool	pool	wooed	cooed	shooed	suit	Luke	food	stewed
full	pull	wood	could	should	soot	look	foot	stood

D. *Now we have four pairs of words on the tape. The same feature of pronunciation differentiates the first word from the second in each pair. What is it? Can you spell all the words? Do you know what they mean?*

Answers: C. fool pull wood cooed should suit Luke foot stewed
D. The first word of each pair ends in a voiced consonant sound, therefore the vowel is long. These were the words: rude, root prove, proof lose, loose bruise, Bruce

DIALOGUE 44. Miss Woodfull'll be furious!

RACHEL: 'How much wood would a woodpecker peck if a woodpecker could peck wood?' Goodness, that's difficult!
MABEL: Looks a good book. Let me have a look?
RACHEL: It's full of puzzles, and riddles, and—
MABEL: Let me look, Rachel!
RACHEL: Mabel! You are awful! You just *took* it!
MABEL: I asked if I could have a look. Now push off. I'm looking at the book.
RACHEL: You're a horrible bully!
MABEL: And you're just a miserable pudding!
RACHEL: I should've kept it in my room.
MABEL: Oh shush, for goodness' sake! Anyway, I shouldn't have thought you could have understood the book, you're so backward.
RACHEL: You're hateful! Give me my book! Oh careful, Mabel! It's Miss Woodfull's book. I'll get into terrible trouble if you—oh *look*! you are *awful*! She'll be *furious*!
MABEL: Well, you shouldn't have pulled, should you?

45. [ɜː] birth, girl

This is a vowel that is very often mispronounced. People purse their lips or make the sound right at the back of the mouth because there is a vowel in their own mother tongue which they confuse with the English sound. Always listen *very* carefully to the tape and when you are trying to imitate the sounds on it, deliberately make your mother tongue sounds and try to hear the difference between the two.
To pronounce this sound correctly, say [ə], then tense the muscles under the jaw and in the tongue, being careful to keep the lips in a neutral position, neither spread wide nor pursed up in a bud. There is far more vibration than for 'shwa' and the vowel is long.

PRACTICE

A.

(a)

her	perfect	stir	bird	turn	further
pert	allergic	fir	birch	burn	turtle
perch	superb	firm	chirp	hurt	absurd
were	person	squirm	circle	murmur	disturbing
prefer	permanent	circus	thirsty	murder	purpose
word	work	earn	early	adjourn	amateur
worm	worse	heard	earth	journey	connoisseur
world	Worthing	search	rehearsal	courtesy	masseur
myrrh	Colonel	*and the exclamation* 'Ugh!'			
myrtle	attorney				

(b) It's the early bird that catches the worm.
A bird in the hand is worth two in the bush.
One good turn deserves another.
First come, first served.
Even a worm will turn.

B. *[ə]* or *[ɜː]? The question to decide is—is the syllable stressed or not? Mark the [ɜː] (stressed) syllables and underline the [ə] (unstressed).*

(a) Bertha preferred to turn to the Colonel whenever it was her turn to rehearse.
(b) Bert and Jemima had a perfectly murderous journey from Hurlingham to Surbiton on Thursday.
(c) Turn down the first turning after the church—or the third, if you prefer.
(d) We've searched for work all over the world, cursing the ever-worsening conditions for labourers.

C. *Which words in the dialogue have to be* ***linked****? Join them up like this:*
. . . this‿early

Answers: B. (a) Bértha preférred to túrn to the Cólonel whenever it was hér túrn to reheárse.
(b) Bért and Jemima had a pérfectly múrderous jóurney from Húrlingham to Súrbiton on Thúrsday.
(c) Túrn down the fírst turning after the church—or the thírd if you prefér.
(d) We've séarched for wórk all over the wórld, cúrsing the ever-wórsening conditions for labourers.
C. this‿early . . . think‿I'm . . . turn‿on . . . world's astir . . . that‿even the worms‿are . . . for‿a worm . . . I'm‿allergic . . . search‿under . . . trees‿and . . . the‿earth . . . and‿I'll . . . with a . . . firm‿ earthworm . . . What‿an . . . wish‿I . . . find‿it . . . so‿early . . . prefer‿a . . . I'm‿a . . . with‿a . . . Er—I'd . . . the early . . . so‿I've heard!

DIALOGUE 45. How's my pert little turtledove?

1ST BIRD: How's my pert little turtledove this early, pearly, murmuring morn?
2ND BIRD: I think I'm worse. I can't turn on my perch. And I'm permanently thirsty—burning, burning. It's murder.
1ST BIRD: My poor, hurt bird. The world's astir. I've heard that even the worms are turning. A worm! You yearn for a worm!
2ND BIRD: I'm *allergic* to worms. Ugh! Dirty, squirming worms!
1ST BIRD: I'll search under the fir trees and the birches, I'll circle the earth—and I'll return with a superb *firm* earthworm for my perfect turtledove.
2ND BIRD: What an absurd bird! You're very chirpy, Sir. I wish I were. All this fervid verse. I find it disturbing so early. I prefer a less wordy bird.
1ST BIRD: No further word, then. I'm a bird with a purpose. Er—I'd better fly; it's the early bird that catches the worm—or so I've heard!

46. Rhythm again (mixed)

In Unit 12 we learnt about rhythm, and practised two very regular patterns: TUM ti TUM and TUM ti ti TUM. The dialogue was made easy because each person used only *one* rhythm throughout. This, of course, is unusual, to say the least. In this unit, the rhythms of conversation are more natural, with each person using a mixture of patterns. However, the *speed* has been kept constant throughout, which means that *all* the stresses come at regular intervals of time. When you feel confident enough, you can practise varying the speed from phrase to phrase to make it all more dramatic and interesting to listen to. But remember, keep the rhythm constant within each phrase.

Banánas and mílk! (slow and surprised)
Thát doesn't soúnd very slímming (faster, amused)

You should now be able to make use of all the aids to fluency that we have covered—linking, weakening, elision, etc.—so that you can work up an almost native-speaker speed!

PRACTICE

A. *Three nursery rhymes to keep you tapping:*

(a) To márket, to márket,
To búy a fat píg.
Hóme again, hóme again,
Jíggety jíg.

To márket, to márket,
To búy a fat hóg.
Hóme again, hóme again,
Jóggety jóg.

(b) Húmpty Dúmpty sát on a wáll,
Húmpty Dúmpty hád a great fáll.
Áll the King's hórses, and áll the King's mén,
Cóuldn't put Húmpty togéther agáin.

(c) Líttle Bo Péep
Has lóst her shéep,
And dóesn't know whére to fínd thém.
Léave them alóne
And théy'll come hóme,
Wágging their táils behínd thém.

B. *Can you put stress marks in these two?*

(a) Sing a song of sixpence
A pocket full of rye,
Four and twenty blackbirds
Baked in a pie.

When the pie was opened
The birds began to sing,
Wasn't that a dainty dish
To set before the King?

(b) Solomon Grundy
Born on Monday
Christened on Tuesday
Married on Wednesday
Fell ill on Thursday
Worse on Friday
Died on Saturday
Buried on Sunday
And that was the end
of Solomon Grundy.

Answers: B. (a) Síng a sóng of síxpénce
A pócket fúll of rýe,
Fóur and twénty bláckbírds
Báked ín a píe.

Whén the píe was ópéned
The bírds begán to síng,
Wásn't thát a dáinty dísh
To sét befóre the Kíng?

(b) Sólomon Grúndy
Bórn on Mónday
Chrístened on Túesday
Márried on Wédnesday
Féll íll on Thúrsday
Wórse on Fríday
Díed on Sáturday
Búried on Súnday
And thát was the énd
Of Sólomon Grúndy.

DIALOGUE 46. Looking for something pretty

SALESGIRL: Good mórning, mádam. Can I hélp you at áll?
ANNABEL: Well, I'm lóoking for a dréss. Sómething to wéar at the théatre. Sómething *prétty*.
SALESGIRL: Cértainly, mádam. Do you knów what síze you áre?
ANNABEL: Well, I *wás* 18́ but I've lóst a lót of wéight since Chrístmas. I've béen on a díet of banánas and mílk.
SALESGIRL: Banánas and mílk! Thát doesn't sóund very slímming. Woúld it be a góod idéa if I tóok your méasurements?
ANNABEL: I féel about a síze 14́! And lóok! That's just what I wánted. That pínk and prímrose chíffon!
SALESGIRL: I háte to téll you, mádam, but you're stíll size 18́. Dón't you thínk sómething a líttle more táilored?

47. [əʊ] coat, code

The sound that we find in words like ‘hole’, ‘boat’, ‘comb’ is not a single sound, but a combination of two—a *DIPHTHONG*.
With the vowel diphthongs (the word ‘diphthong’ is used only of vowels) which we practise in Units 47 to 50, it is the *first* sound that is dominant, unlike the consonant [tʃ] and [dʒ] in which the voice slides quickly to the *second* sound.
All diphthongs are long sounds. When saying [əʊ], hold on to the ‘shwa’ sound a little longer than you normally would in weakened syllables but not as long as if it was [ɜː], then push the lips in one sliding movement forward almost but not quite to the position for saying [uː]. If you do want to lengthen the whole vowel sound for any reason—for instance in calling ‘Hell-o-o-o’—remember it is the [ə] that you lengthen, sliding towards [uː] as you finish. This sound, in fact, has many pronunciations in English, even within the British Isles, but because of the tendency of most languages to pronounce the letter ‘o’ as a single, far more open sound, it is best to aim for a fairly closed [əʊ] in order to combat this.

PRACTICE

A.

so	hero	know	boat	old	hope
go	studio	row	load	told	bone
toe	volcano	yellow	coal	revolt	rose
roll	control	fo(l)k	own	both	poet
stroll	patrol	yo(l)k	grown	sloth	stoic
swollen	enrol	Ho(l)born	(k)nown	quoth	heroic
over	opal	global	cosy	ocean	linoleum
clover	local	notable	pony	closure	custodian
Dover	total	Roman	Toby	soldier	(p)neumonia

ghost	hostess	don't	rogue	dough	mouldy	sew
most	postage	won't	vogue	though	shoulder	Shrewsbury

comb	clothes	gross	Polish	soul	mauve

No difference in pronunciation:

sow – sew	role – roll	bold – bowled
sole – soul	yoke – yolk	mown – moan

B. (a) Won't you row the old boat over the ocean from Dover to Stow-in-the-Wold if I load it with gold?
No, no, I won't row the old boat over the ocean from Dover to Stow-in-the-Wold if you load it with gold.
(b) Won't you show Joan where you're going to grow a whole row of roses when you've sold her those potatoes and tomatoes?
No, no, I won't . . .
(c) Won't you blow your noble Roman nose before you pose for your photo tomorrow?
No, no, I won't . . .

C. *Let's look at the **Tonic** again. In Miss Jones's first speech she mentions the goat and the roses. So when Toby talks about them he stresses the word **'eat'** and in his second sentence **'most things'**. Then Miss Jones says, 'The goat and the roses **both** had to . . .'. It is new information that is stressed. Underline the Tonic in each sentence in the dialogue.*

Answers: C. into the boat . . . won't eat the roses . . . most things . . . boatman so . . . oh no . . . the roses both . . . a rowing boat . . . going to row? . . . too slow . . . motor mower . . . to the boat . . . you see . . . motor boat . . . the boat go? . . . a bit low . . . And the postman . . . Oh no . . . no room . . . by road . . . to snow.

DIALOGUE 47. No wonder the boat was low!

MISS JONES: So the boatman put the goat and the roses and the load of coal into the boat—

TOBY: I hope the goat won't eat the roses. Goats eat most things, you know, Miss Jones.

MISS JONES: They told the boatman so. But oh no, the goat and the roses both had to go in the boat.

TOBY: Was it a rowing boat, Miss Jones? Was the boatman going to row?

MISS JONES: No, they told the boatman rowing would be too slow. So the postman sold him an old motor mower and he roped it to the boat. And so, you see, Toby, he had a motor boat.

TOBY: Did the boat go?

MISS JONES: It was a bit low, with the goat and the coal and the roses and the boatman—

TOBY: *And* the postman and Rover, I suppose—

MISS JONES: Oh no, there was no room for the postman and Rover. They went home by road. And then it began to snow . . .

48. [aʊ] about, aloud

This diphthong begins half-way between the sounds [ʌ] and [ɑː]. If in doubt, begin by saying [ʌ] and you will find that the mere fact of having to push your mouth forward towards [uː] will slightly darken the sound. As with [əʊ], the first sound is the dominant one and the second is not really reached at all.
When you are practising diphthongs, do look at yourself in the mirror and **make sure** that you are sliding very clearly from one sound to the other.

PRACTICE

A.

(a)

how	brown	house	round	fountain
now	town	thousand	bound	mountain
cow	crown	trousers	sound	bouncy
owl	towel	loud	out	plou(gh)
growl	vowel	proud	about	Slou(gh)
fowl	bowel	cloud	shout	bou(gh)

south, mouth, thou, dou(b)t, drou(gh)t, Mao, gaucho

(b) To be down and out.
Ne'er cast a clout till May is out.
They've eaten me out of house and home.
To make a mountain out of a molehill.
You can't make a silk purse out of a sow's ear.
Out and about.
When in doubt, leave it out.

B. *Recognition*

(a) *Which of these are [aʊ] and which are [əʊ]?*

1. I had a terrible **row** with my mother-in-law and now she won't speak to me.
2. We went for a long **row** in Jonathan's boat—I did most of the rowing!
3. As soon as the spring comes I'm going to **sow** all those seeds you gave me.
4. Look at that **sow**! She's got 16 piglets!
5. How old were you when you learned to tie a **bow**?
6. Heavens! Shall I have to **bow** when I'm presented to the Queen?

(b) *Which words are pronounced [aʊ]?*

1. mound mould	2. rouse rows	3. rough bough	4. blouse browse
5. know now	6. grown crown	7. boundary poultry	8. blow below
9. bowl bowel	10. allow yellow	11. down own	12. toward towel

Answers: B. (a) 1. [aʊ] 2. [əʊ] 3. [əʊ] 4. [aʊ] 5. [əʊ] 6. [aʊ]
(b) 1. mound 2. rouse, rows (= fights) 3. bough 4. blouse, browse 5. now 6. crown
7. boundary 8. Neither 9. bowel 10. allow 11. down 12. towel

DIALOGUE 48. Howard's found an owl

HOWARD: Brownie, if you vow not to make a sound, I'll show you an owl that I've found.

BROWNIE: An owl? You've found an owl?

HOWARD: Don't shout so loud. We don't want a crowd to gather round the house. Tie that hound up outside the cowshed. He's so bouncy and he's bound to growl.

BROWNIE: There. I've wound his lead round the plough. No amount of bouncing will get him out now.

HOWARD: Now, not a sound. It's down by the fountain where the cows browse.

BROWNIE: Wow, Howard! It's a brown mountain owl! It's worth about a thousand pounds down in the town.

HOWARD: No doubt. But *my* proud owl is homeward bound—south to the Drowned Mouse Mountains.

49. [eɪ], [aɪ], [ɔɪ] late, lazy; write, ride; voice, boys

Like the two preceding phonemes, the three sounds practised in this unit are diphthongs, but whereas sounds 47 and 48 slid towards the sound [uː] these slide towards [ɪ], once again stopping short just before they reach the second sound. Perhaps it would be more accurate to say that the second sound is [j], but if you practise the diphthongs like this: [ej], [aj], [ɔːj], you must be very careful not to let any air escape after the [j] or you will find that you have added a 'shwa' [ə].
The first diphthong, [eɪ], begins with a slightly more closed sound than the [e] in 'head' and 'bed'.
The second, [aɪ], begins with [ʌ], but the muscles are slightly tensed and there is a bleating quality about it, as in [æ].
The third, [ɔɪ], begins with [ɔː], as in 'born' and 'taught'.

PRACTICE

A. (a) *[eɪ]*

way	name	brain	inflation		male—mail
say	James	chain	patience		sale—sail
parade	estimate (v)	creative	baby	chaos	Gaelic
lemonade	separate (v)	dative	lady	archaic	Israel
bacon	famous	able	acre	angel	waste
potato	fatal	ladle	sacred	ancient	pastry
bathe	change	bass	ache	campaign	champagne
veil	reindeer	weigh	neighbour	eight	reign
dahlia	straight	gauge	gaol	ha(lf)penny	
loan words –	fête	suède	ballet	bouquet	matinée

(b) *[aɪ]*

by	die	kind	silent	rise – rising	
fly	lie	blind	licence	time – timing	
bicycle	Niagara	bible	I'll	i(s)land	sigh
triangle	diameter	idle	while	vi(s)count	thigh
right	sign	neither	rhyme	child	ai(s)le
fight	design	eiderdown	style	wild	Hawaii
cycle	buy	height	Epstein	Ruislip	ninth
Cyprus	guy	sleight	Einstein	disguise	pint
Michael	maestro	eye	Christ	clim(b)	

(c) *[ɔɪ]*

boy	royal	noise	oil	ointment	lawyer
buoy	employer	voice	boil	poignant	Sawyer
enjoy	oyster	join	toil	avoid	

B. To make hay while the sun shines.
The blind leading the blind.
A stitch in time saves nine.
An apple a day keeps the doctor away.
A cat has nine lives.
Out of sight, out of mind.
To spoil the ship for a ha'p'orth (a halfpennyworth) of tar.

C. Boys and girls come out to play.
The moon is shining bright as day.
Leave your supper and leave your sleep,
And join your playfellows in the street.

This is the grave of Mike O'Day,
Who died maintaining his right of way.
His right was clear, his will was strong—
But he's just as dead as if he'd been wrong.

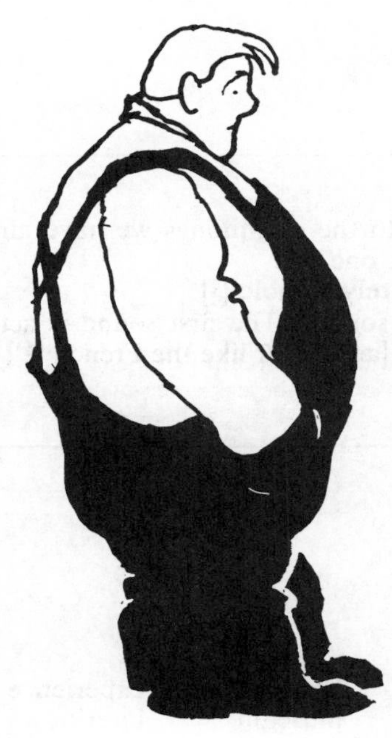

DIALOGUE 49. James Doyle and the boilermakers' strike

OLD GENTLEMAN: I say! Boy! What's all that frightful noise?
BOY: It's the boilermakers from Tyneside. They're on strike. I'm on my way to join them.
OLD GENTLEMAN: You a boilermaker?
BOY: Me? No, I slave for United Alloys. But I'll add my voice to anyone fighting for his rights.
OLD GENTLEMAN: Wait! Why are they striking this time?
BOY: A rise in wages mainly—and overtime for nights.
OLD GENTLEMAN: Why don't they use their brains? A rise in pay means rising prices and greater inflation. What's the point? Who gains?
BOY: That's blackmail, mate. There's high unemployment in Tyneside and the employers exploit the situation. They pay a highly trained boilermaker starvation wages. It's a disgrace.
OLD GENTLEMAN: What's your name?
BOY: James Doyle. I come from a line of fighters. My Aunt Jane chained herself to the railings in 1908. She was quite famous.
OLD GENTLEMAN: I shall be highly annoyed if you tie yourself to mine!

50. [ɪə], [eə] pierce, beard; scarce, stairs

These two diphthongs both move towards [ə]. As with the diphthongs we have already practised, the dominant sound is in both cases the first one.
The first diphthong, [ɪə], slides from [ɪ] to [ə] via a barely audible [j].
In the second, [eə], there is no [j] between the two sounds. The first sound is actually more open than [e]—in fact, half-way between [e] and [æ], rather like the French 'è', as in 'mère'.

PRACTICE

A.

(a) *[ɪə]*

ear	here	queer	Piers	Lyceum	experience
beard	mere	beer	fierce	museum	interior
weary	we're	eerie	frontier	Colosseum	mysterious
hero	era	peony	European	Algeria	pianist
zero	Vera	theory	Korean	Siberia	Ian
peer	spear	weird	theatre	skier	diarrhoea
pier	sphere	Madeira			

(b) *[eə]*

air	fairy	care	Mary	librarian	bear
lair	dairy	stare	vary	vegetarian	pear
stair	prairie	beware	canary	aquarium	swear
millionaire		player	parent	mayor	bolero
questionnaire		prayer	Sarah	conveyor	sombrero
air	there	wear	scarce	aeroplane	harum-scarum
heir	they're	where			
e'er	their				

(c) Here today, gone tomorrow.
He that hath ears to hear, let him hear.
Here, here!
There's none so queer as folk.
All the world is queer save thee and me—and even thee's a little queer.

All's fair in love and war.
Share and share alike.
Hair of the dog that bit you.
If the cap fits, wear it.

Fair's fair.
There, there!
As mad as a March hare.
To bear a grudge.

Mary, Mary, quite contrary.

What is this life if,
Full of care,
We have no time
To stand and stare.

50 (cont.). [aɪə], [aʊə] fire, tired; flower, our

These two are really triphthongs, but in both cases you slide so rapidly from the first sound to the third that the middle one is hardly heard at all. For instance, the word 'fireworks', when said quickly, sounds like [fʌːwɜːks], 'for hours and hours' comes out as [frɑːzənɑːz]. Diphthongs and triphthongs are usually pronounced as single syllables.
N.B. 'vowel', 'bowel', 'towel', 'trowel', are all pronounced [aʊl] like 'growl', 'fowl', etc. You do not hear the 'w'. They are all words of one syllable. Some people do pronounce the [ʊ] sound before the dark [ɫ], but this is not necessary. At all events, do not give this so much strength that it becomes another syllable.

PRACTICE

A.

(a) *[aɪə]*

fire	tired	siren	empire	crier	briar
hire	inspired	spiral	umpire	pliers	liar
admire	acquired	virus	vampire	fiery	diary
diagram	giant	diet	science	violet	tyre
dialogue	defiant	quiet	scientist	violent	flyer
diamond	psychiatry	society	client	violin	higher
lion	prior	Ireland	biro	Byron	wiry
Zion	riot	iron	giro	tyrant	enquiry
Maria	Brian	Messiah	choir		
via	bias				
wire	hire	byre	lyre		
why're	higher	buyer	liar		

(b) *[aʊə]*

sour	tower	cowering	flowery	nowadays
scour	shower	towering	showery	allowance
devour	power	devouring		ploughable
Howard	dowry		our	flour
coward	cowrie	how're	hour	flower

(c) There's no smoke without fire.
The lion may lie down with the lamb.
Diamonds are a girl's best friend.

The burnt child dreads the fire.
To rule with a rod of iron.

Flower power.
Enough to make the milk turn sour.
'I count only the hours that are serene' (*on a sundial*).

To be a tower of strength.

B. *Which is s/he saying?*

(a) 1. Oh dear, I don't like the look of that beer. / bear.

2. My dear, you've got a tear / tear on the front of your skirt. [ɪə] / [eə]

3. We really / rarely go to the cinema every week.

4. This place is very eerie. / airy.

(b) 1. Her father's going to give her a large diary. / dowry.

2. How would you describe a viol? / vowel?

3. You've got a buyer / bower—how marvellous!

4. Take care—it's hired! / Howard!

5. Do you know what those tyres / towers are for?

C. (a) *Which word goes where?*

wear/where — 1. . . . are you going to . . . that?
they're/there/their — 2. You mean . . . really going to take . . . aunt . . . ?

(b) *If we number the four diphthongs in this unit ([ɪə] = 1, [eə] = 2, [aɪə] = 3, [aʊə] = 4), can you put the correct number by each of the following names?*

a) Mary ( ) d) Brian ( ) g) Vera ( ) j) Ian ( ) m) Sarah ( )
b) Orion ( ) e) Leonie ( ) h) Aaron ( ) k) Byron ( ) n) Piers ( )
c) Lear ( ) f) Howard ( ) i) Maria ( ) l) Dorothea ( ) o) Ryan ( )

D. *Listen to the dialogue. Mark the stressed syllables.*

eerie	mysterious	atmosphere	nobody
hundreds	animal	vampire	everywhere
anywhere	staircase	weary	nearly

Answers: B. (a) 1. beer 2. tear [eə] 3. really 4. eerie
(b) 1. dowry 2. vowel 3. buyer 4. Howard 5. tyres
C. (a) 1. Where are you going to wear that?
2. You mean they're really going to take their aunt there?
(b) a) 2 b) 3 c) 1 d) 3 e) 1 f) 4 g) 1 h) 2 i) 3 j) 1 k) 3 l) 1 m) 2 n) 1 o) 3
D. éerie mystérious átmosphere nóbody
húndreds ánimal vámpire éverywhere
ánywhere stáircase wéary néarly

DIALOGUE 50. It's eerie in here

AARON: Oh Piers, it's eerie in here—there's a sort of mysterious atmosphere—as if nobody's been here for years.

PIERS: That's queer. Look, Aaron—over there. There's a weird light, like hundreds of pairs of eyes staring. I think we're in some animal's lair.

AARON: Where?

PIERS: There. They're coming nearer. My God, Aaron, they're giant bats.

AARON: Oh no! I can feel them in my hair. They're tearing my beard! I can't bear it, Piers.

PIERS: What if they're vampires? They're everywhere. Let's get out of here. We could try and climb higher.

AARON: No fear! I'm not going anywhere, I'm staying here.

PIERS: Aaron! There's a kind of iron staircase. Over here. Only take care. There's a sheer drop.
(*Sounds of panting*)

AARON: God, I'm weary. We must have been climbing these stairs for hours.

PIERS: Cheer up, Aaron, I can see a square of light and smell fresh air and flowers. We're nearly there!

51. Intonation 1: The rise–fall pattern (statements, 'wh-' questions)

Stress, rhythm and intonation are, if anything, more important for communication than the correct pronunciation of individual sounds. We have looked at intonation when we saw how meaning could be altered by shifting the Tonic.

The Tonic is the syllable of greatest stress within an utterance. It is also the syllable where most 'movement' occurs.

A sentence with the Tonic at the end will look like this, the voice rising on each stressed syllable and then falling slightly below the pitch it was at before:

'A farmer went trotting upon his grey mare.'

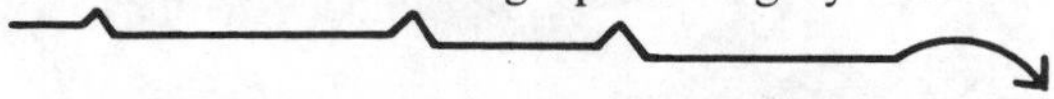

The whole sentence seems to be dropping like a series of small waterfalls towards the Tonic, in which all the features of the other stressed syllables—movement, loudness, length—are present in an exaggerated form.

This is called the 'rise–fall' intonation pattern. If the Tonic is the last syllable in the sentence, the voice will slide from high to low *within that syllable*.

I bought some food.  Jane's away.

If there are one or more unstressed syllables after the Tonic, the voice drops on the following syllable and there is no further movement until the end of the phrase or sentence.

I thought I saw a burglar.  I thought I saw an alligator.

This pattern is used (a) for statements
(b) for 'wh-' questions (what, when, where, which, who, whom, whose, why, and—a bit of a cheat—how).

There is also a plain 'falling' pattern, in which the voice does not rise on the Tonic but remains flat and then falls either within the final syllable or on the following one:

I feel sick. It's snowing.

The difference between this and the first pattern is that if you use the second you will sound distinctly bored or, at the very least, lacking in enthusiasm.

A. *Statements*

(a) *final syllable*
I took the books.
I put them down.
We're going to church.

(b) *second-last syllable*
I've bought you a present.
My father's a teacher.
We're going by taxi.

(c) *followed by several syllables*
I've dropped the thermometer.
He's going into politics.
I think he's an anthropologist.

B. *'wh-' questions*

(a) What's that?
Where's the tea?
Which is yours?
Who's that girl?
Whose are these?

(b) What are you doing?
When did you get here?
Where are you going?
Why didn't you tell me?
How are the children?

(c) When will you finish it?
Which is the easiest?
Who were you talking to?
Why don't we go to the cinema?
How did you hurt yourself?

C. *Practise making a difference between rise–fall and falling intonation*

It's raining.
I'm going away.
I'm ill.
I've killed him.

DIALOGUE 51. What time does the plane leave?

ROBERT: What's the time?
EMILY: Ten past two, dear.
ROBERT: When does the plane leave?
EMILY: Not until a quarter to four.
ROBERT: Why did we get here so early?
EMILY: Because you said we must allow plenty of time for traffic jams and accidents.
ROBERT: Where's my briefcase? What have you done with my briefcase?
EMILY: It's there, dear, between your feet.
ROBERT: Emily! Where are you going?
EMILY: I'm going to ask that gentleman what they were announcing over the loudspeaker.
ROBERT: Which gentleman?
EMILY: That man over there with all the packages.
ROBERT: Who is he?
EMILY: I don't know. But he looked as though he was listening to the announcement . . . Yes, I was afraid so. The plane's delayed. It won't be leaving till five.
ROBERT: How did *he* manage to hear it if we didn't?
EMILY: Because he was listening. You were talking too much to hear.
ROBERT: What do you mean, I was talking too much?
EMILY: Oh dear. Never mind.
ROBERT: What time is it now, Emily?

52. Intonation 2: The fall–rise pattern (yes/no questions, requests for repetition, greetings)

This pattern is the reverse of the one we looked at in Unit 51. The main movement in the sentence is still on the Tonic syllable, but this time the voice *falls* on the Tonic and then *rises*. You use this pattern to ask questions that require an answer of 'Yes' or 'No'.
Let's look at three sentences, first as statements with a rise–fall pattern, and then in question form:

(a) I bought some food. (b) Did you buy some food?
I saw a burglar. Did you see a burglar?
I saw an alligator. Did you see an alligator?

Did you notice that the second pattern is, in fact, not the *exact* reverse of the first? In the statement, once the voice has fallen after the Tonic, it stays at the same level, but in the question the voice continues to rise to the end of the sentence. Be careful not to rise too sharply, especially if you have a lot to add after the Tonic, or you'll end up in a squeak!

Did you see an alligator in the bath at the party last night?

The fall–rise pattern is also used for greetings, the voice rising and falling on the greeting, and then, on the name that follows, falling a little more and rising again sharply.

Hullo, Jane! Good evening, Mrs Baker!

You also use this tune with 'wh-' questions when you're asking for information to be repeated. The intonation here usually expresses shock or anger, implying, 'I don't believe you!'

I saw your girlfriend at the cinema last night.
Where did you see her?
At the cinema. She was with Charlie Brown.
Who was she with? Charlie Brown?

PRACTICE

A. *Yes/no questions*

Are you alone?
Can I come in?
May I sit down?
Do you mind if I smoke?
Are you sure?
Have you got an ashtray?
May I borrow some matches?
Would it be possible to have a cup of tea?
Oh, am I being a nuisance?

B. *Greetings*

Hullo, Peter.
Good morning, Doctor.
Good afternoon, Mr Mumble.
Good evening, everybody.

C. *Requests for repetition*

What did you say?
When was all this?
Where did you say you found it?
Which pills did you take?
Who did you say you went with?
Whose wife danced on the table?
Why did you think it was me?
How did you get in?

DIALOGUE 52. Were you at home last night?

SERGEANT: Good evening, Sir. Mr Holmes?
HOLMES: Good evening, officer. Yes, that's right—John Holmes. Won't you come in?
SERGEANT: Thank you. May I ask you a few questions?
HOLMES: Yes, of course. Won't you sit down?
SERGEANT: Thank you. It's about last night. Were you at home, Mr Holmes?
HOLMES: Yes, Sergeant, I was, actually. I wasn't feeling very well.
SERGEANT: Were you alone?
HOLMES: Er, yes. My wife had gone to the cinema with a friend.
SERGEANT: Did *you* go out at all?
HOLMES: No, I stayed in all evening—that is, except for a few minutes when I popped out to post a letter.
SERGEANT: Do you remember what time this was?
HOLMES: Yes, it was about—um—half past eight.
SERGEANT: What time did you say? Half past eight? Anybody see you when you—er—popped out for 5 minutes to post your letter?
HOLMES: No, I don't think so. Oh yes, just a minute. The caretaker said 'good evening'.
SERGEANT: The caretaker, Mr Holmes? Mr Holmes, the caretaker was murdered last night.

53. Intonation 3: Combined patterns (pausing in the middle, lists, doubt, apology, etc.)

Intonation is one of the means a speaker uses to send signals to the listener, such as 'Don't interrupt me; I haven't finished yet,' or 'That's all for the moment. Over to you.' If the speaker pauses in the middle of a sentence, he will stop on a *rising* tone to show you that he intends to continue.

I was about to put my hand inside the box . . . when I heard a ticking noise.

In the first part of the sentence, up to the pause, the pattern is the ordinary rise–fall one of statements, until you come to the Tonic, which has the fall–rise tune. This fall–rise only on the Tonic is frequently used to express doubt, hesitation or apology. It can also imply, 'Can I help you?'

Well . . . I'm sorry. I think I've got it. Dr Mark's secretary.

You use the fall–rise tune, too, when enumerating lists. Every item on your list will have its own pattern, each one on the same level as the last:

Monday, Tuesday, Wednesday . . .

If your list is complete, the final item will have the rise–fall pattern, indicating to your listener that that's the lot. This is called a 'closed' list:

I'm free on Monday, Tuesday, Wednesday, Thursday.

If you want to show that you *could* go on but leave the rest to your listener's imagination, you use the fall–rise pattern on the last item as well. This is called an 'open' list:

I'm free on Monday, Tuesday, Wednesday, Thursday . . .

implying that any day of the week is possible. This applies to questions, too:

Are you free on Monday or Tuesday or Wednesday or Thursday?

Are you free on Monday or Tuesday or Wednesday or Thursday . . . ?

PRACTICE

A. (a) If you go to India / you must see the Taj Mahal.
I've bought a painting / but now I don't like it.
I saw your uncle in the park / but I don't think he saw me.

(b) Yes. No. Excuse me. Williams' Bakery.
I don't think so. I'm sorry to bother you. Mandrake College.

B. (a) *Closed lists—statements and questions*

We went to Rome and Athens and Beirut and Cairo.
I can offer you tea or coffee or hot chocolate.
Did you see my cousin or my uncle or my aunt?
Shall we go to the cinema or the pub or stay at home?

(b) *Open lists*
Now say the sentences in B (a) again, using the fall–rise intonation on the last item as well.

DIALOGUE 53. I'm afraid I think I'm lost

OLD LADY: Excuse me. I'm terribly sorry to bother you . . .
POLICEMAN: Yes? That's quite all right. Can I help you at all?
OLD LADY: I don't know how to begin.
POLICEMAN: Well, the beginning's always a good place to start.
OLD LADY: But, you see, I don't know the beginning. I'm looking for a small, old-fashioned hotel where I—if only I could remember the name!
POLICEMAN: Or the name of the street?
OLD LADY: The *street*? Oh, I've no *idea*, I'm afraid.
POLICEMAN: Or the area?
OLD LADY: I know it was not far from the Pier. Or could that have been *last* year, I wonder? No, no, last year I went with Emily—I think.
POLICEMAN: Did you say near the Pier? There's no pier here.
OLD LADY: There *must* be! My hotel was near it.
POLICEMAN: Which pier?
OLD LADY: Eastbourne Pier, of course!
POLICEMAN: Eastbourne? But this is Seaford!
OLD LADY: Seaford! Really? I thought it seemed rather a long way!

54. Intonation 4: Tag questions

Tag questions are those little questions stuck at the end of a sentence, usually asking for confirmation of what has just been said.

In the first pattern the speaker makes a statement which he or she believes to be true. The tag question is not really asking a question—the speaker does not expect anything but agreement.

You're learning English, aren't you?
Yes, I am.

The sentence, being a statement, will have a rise–fall intonation pattern, *and so will the tag question*:

You're learning English, aren't you? You killed Cock Robin, didn't you?

In the second pattern the speaker is not at all sure of the truth of his statement. In fact, though it has a statement form, it is really a question, so it will have a fall–rise intonation, *and so will the tag question*:

You didn't eat it, did you? She will be there tonight, won't she?

The third pattern starts by making a definite statement. The speaker seems certain that it's true. Then there comes a slight pause, as if an awful feeling of doubt is creeping in. The tag question expresses this doubt with a fall–rise intonation:

That's *my* money—isn't it? You said you wanted to go to Aden—didn't you?

Two things to note:

(a) If the main sentence is in the affirmative, the tag question is always in the negative. If the main sentence is in the negative, the tag question is in the affirmative.
(b) Although there's a comma before the tag question you *link* if the question itself begins with a vowel:
That's the answer, isn't it? I'm not going to fall, am I?

PRACTICE

A. *Rise–fall*
This is your frog, isn't it?
You know where I found it, don't you?
And *you* put it in my bed, didn't you?
So you know what's going to happen to you, don't you?
And you won't do it again, will you?

B. *Fall–rise*
You'll come with me to the school fête, won't you?
I'll pick you up at two, shall I?
And we'll go by car, shall we?
We won't have to stay long, will we?
You'll come and have some tea afterwards, won't you?

C. *Definite statement followed by doubt—rise–fall, fall–rise*
You have got the tickets—haven't you?
I did turn off the bath water—didn't I?
The hotel is in this street—isn't it?
You weren't in that plane crash—were you?

D. *Tag questions with special stress—rise–fall, fall–rise within the stressed word*
I like pop music—don't *you*?
We're going to the pub on Saturday—aren't *you*?
We've been invited to the Joneses—haven't *you*?
Mine's a real diamond—isn't *yours*?

DIALOGUE 54. Fish like a bit of silence, don't they?

PASSER-BY: Nasty weather, isn't it?
FISHERMAN: All right if you're a duck.
PASSER-BY: Come here regularly, don't you?
FISHERMAN: Yes, I do.
PASSER-BY: Come fishing every Sunday, don't you?
FISHERMAN: That's right.
PASSER-BY: Not many other people today, are there?
FISHERMAN: No there aren't, are there?
PASSER-BY: Caught some fish already, have you?
FISHERMAN: No, not yet.
PASSER-BY: Stay here all day, will you?
FISHERMAN: I should like to.
PASSER-BY: You don't mind if I sit down, do you? My talking doesn't disturb you, does it?
FISHERMAN: No, but it seems to disturb the fish.
PASSER-BY: Ah, they like a bit of silence, don't they? Same as me. I like a bit of peace, too, don't you?

55. Revision 1

Weak forms: out of [əv] the [ðə] car; peas and [ən] carrots and [ən] cabbage.
Linking: sitting‿on‿an‿ant's nest; your bit‿of beef.
Elision: detes(t) picnics; couldn'(t) stay; roas(t) pork.
Two consecutive stresses: stóp grúmbling; brówn bréad; bóiled béef.
Rising intonation of incomplete lists: tomatoes, peppers, lettuce, cucumber, beetroot . . .
And, of course, all the individual *phonemes*.

PRACTICE

A. *A few proverbs*

Eat, drink and be merry, for tomorrow we die.
A red rag to a bull.
There's no smoke without fire.
You can't fit a square peg into a round hole.
Here today, gone tomorrow.
A bull in a china shop.

B. *Which is s/he saying?*

(a) That sounds to me like a foul. / vowel.

(b) We've decided to cover this part with glass. / grass.

(c) What a cat / cad your cousin is!

(d) These sheep are going to have their wool shorn / torn off.

(e) I didn't realise it was so light, / late, did you?

C. *Do you know how the 'o's and 'u's (either separately or in combination) are pronounced in the names of these fruit and vegetables? Put the correct phonetic symbol(s) after each one.*

(a) lemon [ ]
(b) lettuce [ ]
(c) almond [ ]
(d) sultana [ ]
(e) orange [ ]
(f) sweetcorn [ ]
(g) broad bean [ ]
(h) asparagus [ ]
(i) beetroot [ ]
(j) artichoke [ ]
(k) sprout [ ]
(l) walnut [ ]
(m) turnip [ ]
(n) melon [ ]
(o) currant [ ]
(p) grapefruit [ ]
(q) sugarbeet [ ]
(r) gooseberry [ ]
(s) apricot [ ]
(t) carrot [ ]
(u) cucumber [ ] [
(v) potato [ ] [ ]
(w) onion [ ] [ ]
(x) mushroom [ ] [
(y) cauliflower [ ] [

D. *Listen to the dialogue. Mark the stressed syllables.*

detest, basket, indoors, beautiful, cabbage, pudding, perfect, behind, chicken, salad, tomatoes, cucumber, beetroot, rabbit, dumplings

Answers: B. (a) vowel (b) glass (c) cat (d) shorn (e) light
C. (a) [ə] (b) [ɪ] (c) [ə] (d) [ʊ] (e) [ɒ] (f) [ɔː] (g) [ɔː] (h) [ə] (i) [uː] (j) [əʊ] (k) [aʊ] (l) [ʌ] (m) [ɜː] (n) [ə] (o) [ʌ] (p) [uː] (q) [ʊ] (r) [ʊ] (s) [ɒ] (t) [ə] (u) [juː] [ʌ] (v) [ə] [əʊ] (w) [ʌ] [ə] (x) [ʌ] [ʊ] (y) [ɒ] [aʊə]
D. detést, básket, indóors, beaútiful, cábbage, púdding, pérfect, behínd, chícken, sálad, tomátoes, cúcumber, béetroot, rábbit, dúmplings

DIALOGUE 55. A bit of beef at the picnic

PAUL: Picnics! I *detest* picnics!

KATE: Paul, do stop grumbling and get the basket out of the car. We couldn't stay indoors today. It's beautiful!

PAUL: I do like a proper Sunday dinner. What I like is roast pork with apple sauce and gravy, peas and carrots and cabbage, and treacle tart for pudding . . .

KATE: Here's a perfect spot! Spread the rug behind this bush. Good. Look, we've got brown bread and butter and pâté and cold chicken . . .

PAUL: Blast! I'm sitting on an ant's nest! *Picnics!*

KATE: And the salad's got tomatoes, peppers, lettuce, cucumber, beetroot . . .

PAUL: Rabbit food! Oh for a plate of boiled beef and dumplings!

KATE: Oh dear! Paul, I do believe your bit of beef is coming this way! Isn't that a *bull*?

56. Revision 2

Remember:
Weak forms: of [əv], to [tə] and so on.
Linking: that's‿a; sort of; sitting‿in.

Tag questions: you're sitting in, isn't it?; just joking, aren't you?; the plants, can it?
Intonation: rise–fall on statements and 'wh-' questions, fall–rise on 'yes/no' questions.
Syllable stress: make your voice higher and louder and hang on to the syllable a little longer on the stresses.
And, of course,
Rhythm: Feel it, like music. Not the same all the way through, but regular within each phrase.

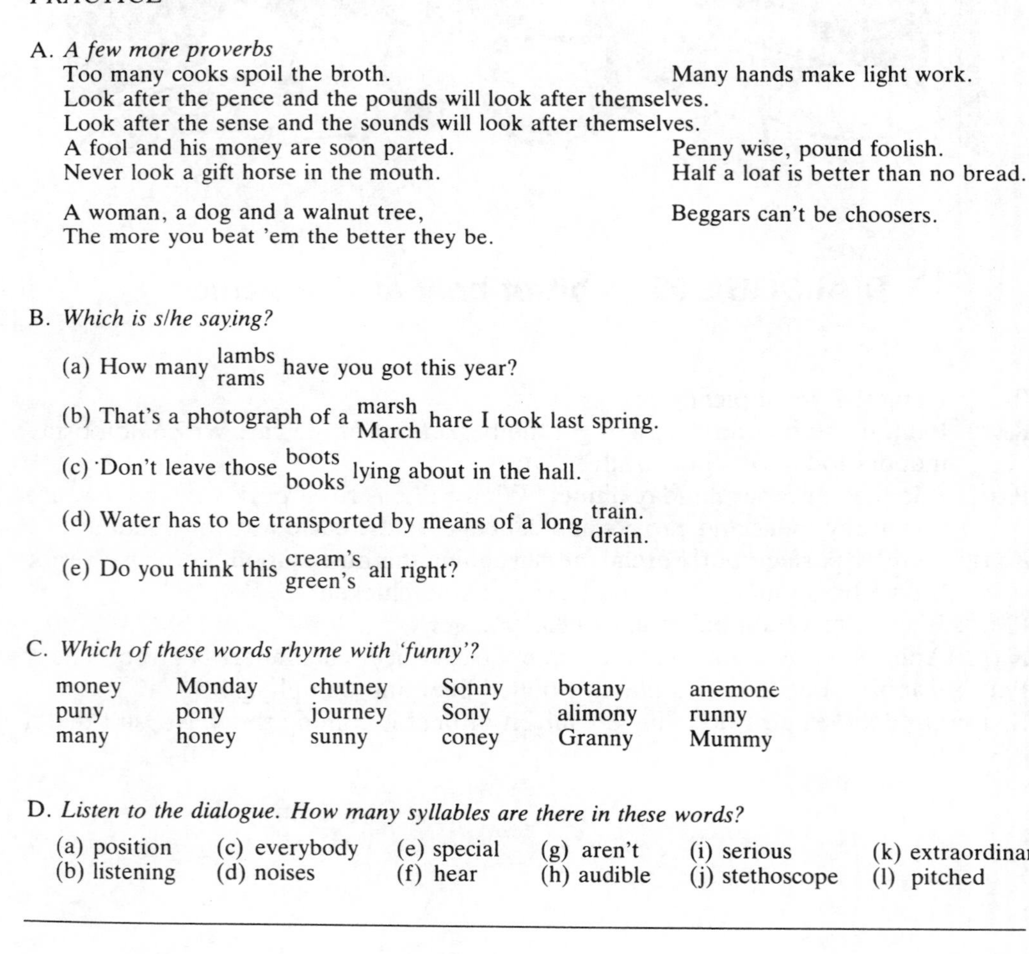

PRACTICE

A. *A few more proverbs*

Too many cooks spoil the broth.
Look after the pence and the pounds will look after themselves.
Look after the sense and the sounds will look after themselves.
A fool and his money are soon parted.
Never look a gift horse in the mouth.

A woman, a dog and a walnut tree,
The more you beat 'em the better they be.

Many hands make light work.
Penny wise, pound foolish.
Half a loaf is better than no bread.
Beggars can't be choosers.

B. *Which is s/he saying?*

(a) How many lambs / rams have you got this year?

(b) That's a photograph of a marsh / March hare I took last spring.

(c) Don't leave those boots / books lying about in the hall.

(d) Water has to be transported by means of a long train. / drain.

(e) Do you think this cream's / green's all right?

C. *Which of these words rhyme with 'funny'?*

money	Monday	chutney	Sonny	botany	anemone
puny	pony	journey	Sony	alimony	runny
many	honey	sunny	coney	Granny	Mummy

D. *Listen to the dialogue. How many syllables are there in these words?*

(a) position	(c) everybody	(e) special	(g) aren't	(i) serious	(k) extraordinary
(b) listening	(d) noises	(f) hear	(h) audible	(j) stethoscope	(l) pitched

Answers: B. (a) rams (b) marsh (c) books (d) drain (e) cream's
C. money, honey, sunny, Sonny, runny
D. (a) 3 (b) 2 (c) 4 (d) 2 (e) 2 (f) 1 (g) 1 (h) 3 (i) 3 (j) 3 (k) 3 (l) 1

DIALOGUE 56. Listening to the plants talking

GEORGE: That's a funny sort of position you're sitting in, isn't it?
ANDREW: I'm listening to the plants talking.
GEORGE: Andrew! Plants can't talk—everybody knows that.
ANDREW: But they make noises. Not noises like the ones human beings make. Not even animal noises. Special sounds. You can hardly hear them with the human ear.
GEORGE: Well, if they aren't audible, how do you *know* they make them? Come on, you're just joking, aren't you?
ANDREW: I'm as serious as . . . as . . . Sunday. Honestly, George. Cross my heart and hope to die.
GEORGE: What's that thing that's hanging round your neck? Looks like a sort of a snake.
ANDREW: It's a doctor's stethoscope. Lie down on the ground and put the stethoscope into your ears. Hear anything?
GEORGE: Golly, I *did*! How extraordinary! A very high-pitched squeaking! It can't be the plants, can it?

57. Revision 3

Stress: no stress on negative prefixes: impolíte; unháppy.
consecutive stresses: goód héavens; bíg bláck béard; mérmáid.
the shifting Tonic: Are you a mérmáid? Of cóurse I'm a mermaid.
Intonation: especially of questions.
Linking: are you‿ʷa; seen‿a; got‿a.
Elision: hasn('t) got time; han(d)some; bi(g) black.
Weak forms: but [bət] are you; handsome and [ən] dashing.
also within words: polite [pəláɪt]; forgive [fəgív]; handsome [hǽnsəm].

PRACTICE

A. *Still more proverbs*

Pride comes before a fall.
One good turn deserves another.
If wishes were horses, then beggars would ride.
If 'ifs' and 'ands' were pots and pans, there'd be no need for tinkers.
Tinker, tailor, soldier, sailor, rich man, poor man, beggarman, thief.

Great minds think alike.
Fools seldom differ.
Nothing venture, nothing gain.

B. *Which is s/he saying?*

(a) The brute! He pinched my shin! / chin! / gin!

(b) I just adore fresh / French bread.

(c) I'll find out if he ever came to the surface / service again.

(d) Have you ever seen such an awful sore / shore / chore / jaw before in all your life?

(e) I'm so cross. I've lost the marvellous cot / cod / cart / card I got from Tom and Margaret.

C. *Underline the Tonic in each phrase or sentence in the following dialogue:*

I'm going to the Repton Show in October.
That's a boat show, isn't it?
No, a motor show.
Are you going to Repton alone?
No, Peter's going, too.
Peter? Peter who? Which Peter?
Peter Blenkinsop. I told you I was going to Repton with Peter.
When did you tell me? It must have been someone else. You never told me.

D. *Before you listen to the dialogue, can you mark the stressed syllables in these words?*

mermaid	before	unhappy	handsome	actually
impolite	upset	borrow	delighted	unadventurous

Answers: B. (a) gin (b) French (c) service (d) shore (e) cod.
C. I'm going to the Repton Show in Oc<u>to</u>ber. That's a <u>boat</u> show, isn't it? No, a <u>mo</u>tor show. Are you going to Repton <u>alone</u>? No, Peter's going, <u>too</u>. Peter? <u>Pe</u>ter <u>who</u>? <u>Which</u> Peter? Peter <u>Blen</u>kinsop. I <u>told</u> you I was going to Repton with Peter. <u>When</u> did you tell me? It must have been someone <u>else</u>. You never told <u>me</u>.
D. mérmaid, impolíte, befóre, upsét, unháppy, bórrow, hándsome, delíghted, áctually, unadvénturous.

DIALOGUE 57. Nobody wants a mermaid

Passer-by: Good heavens! Forgive me, but—are you a mermaid?

Mermaid: Of course I'm a mermaid! You can *see* I'm a mermaid. It's most impolite to stare like that.

Passer-by: I'm terribly sorry. I didn't mean to be rude. Only I've never seen a mermaid before.

Mermaid: (*weeping*) Well, now you have.

Passer-by: Oh dear! I didn't mean to upset you.

Mermaid: It wasn't you. It's just that I'm so unhappy. He doesn't love me.

Passer-by: *Who* doesn't love you? Haven't you got a hankie? No, of course not. How silly of me. Here, borrow mine. That's right. Have a good blow and tell me all about it.

Mermaid: He's a sailor, you see. He's so handsome and dashing with his big black beard and flashing eyes. But he doesn't want a mermaid.

Passer-by: There, there. He ought to be delighted—you can follow him out to sea.

Mermaid: He says he hasn't got time for girls at sea.

Passer-by: Don't you think you'd actually be happier with a nice, quiet, ordinary, unadventurous chap—like me?

58. Extra practice. A few more rhymes and jingles

Georgie Porgie, pudding and pie,
Kissed the girls and made them cry.
When the boys came out to play,
Georgie Porgie ran away.

Diddle diddle dumpling, my son John
Went to bed with his trousers on,
One shoe off and one shoe on,
Diddle diddle dumpling, my son John.

Old King Cole
Was a merry old soul
And a merry old soul was he.
He called for his pipe
And he called for his bowl
And he called for his fiddlers three.

Hey diddle diddle,
The cat and the fiddle,
The cow jumped over the moon.
The little dog laughed
To see such sport
And the dish ran away with the spoon.

Half a pound of twopenny rice,
Half a pound of treacle,
That's the way the money goes.
Pop goes the weasel!

Ring-a-ring o' roses,
A pocketful of posies.
A-tishoo! A-tishoo!
We all fall down.

Little Tommy Tucker
Sings for his supper.
What shall we give him?
Brown bread and butter.

Little Polly Flinders
Sat among the cinders
Warming her pretty little toes.
Her mother came and caught her
And whipped her little daughter
For spoiling her nice new clothes.

I had a little nut tree,
Nothing would it bear
But a silver nutmeg
And a golden pear.
The King of Spain's daughter
Came to visit me
And all for the sake
Of my little nut tree.

Betty Bodder bought some butter.
'But,' she said, 'this butter's bitter.
If I put it in my batter
It will make my batter bitter.'
So she bought a bit of butter
Better than her bitter butter,
And she put it in her batter,
And her batter wasn't bitter.
So 'twas better Betty Bodder bought a bit of better butter!

This is the house that Jack built.
This is the malt that lay in the house that Jack built.
This is the rat that ate the malt that lay in the house that Jack built.

. . . and so on till you end up with:

This is the priest all shaven and shorn
Who married the man all tattered and torn
Who loved the maiden all forlorn
Who milked the cow with the crumpled horn
That tossed the dog
That worried the cat
That chased the rat
That ate the malt
That lay in the house that Jack built!

PRACTICE

A. *Do you know how these words are pronounced?*

although	bought	dough	fought	plough	thorough	through
borough	brought	drought	nought	rough	though	tough
bough	cough	enough	ought	sought	thought	trough

Boroughbridge Loughborough Scarborough Slough

B. *How is the letter 'a' pronounced in English in the names of these places?*

France	Wales	Holland	Portugal	New Zealand
Japan	China	Bulgaria	Malaysia	South Africa
Brazil	Nassau	Uganda	Hungary	Yugoslavia
Spain	Arabia	Albania	Romania	Australia

C. *Here are all the months of the year. Put a stress mark on the stressed syllables.*

January	March	May	July	September	November
February	April	June	August	October	December

D. *Weak forms. Listen to the tape. The speakers are speaking very fast. What are they saying?*

E. *Listen to the intonation patterns.*

A. Hullo, how *are* you?
B. I'm very well. But how are *you*?
A. Why do you ask?
B. I thought you looked ill.
A. What do you mean, ill?
B. You've got spots.
A. Who?
B. You.
A. What spots?
B. Sort of red spots.
A. Where?
B. All over your face.
A. What shall I do?
B. You could always wear a veil.

A. How do you do?
B. How do you do?
A. Haven't we met before?
B. Have we? When?
A. At your cousin's party.
B. Whose cousin?
A. Your cousin.
B. I haven't got a cousin.
A. You must have! We met there!
B. Are you sure it was me?
A. Well, why don't we have a cup of coffee and see if we can find out?

Answers: A.

[ɔːlðə́ʊ]	[bɔːt]	[dəʊ]	[fɔːt]	[plaʊ]	[θʌ́rə]	[θruː]
[bʌ́rə]	[brɔːt]	[draʊt]	[nɔːt]	[rʌf]	[ðəʊ]	[tʌf]
[baʊ]	[kɒf]	[inʌ́f]	[ɔːt]	[sɔːt]	[θɔːt]	[trɒf]

[bʌrəbrɪdʒ] [lʌfbrə] [skɑːbrə] [slaʊ]

B.

[ɑː]	[eɪ]	[ə]	[ʊ]	[iː – ə]
[ə – æ]	[ə]	[eə – ə]	[ə – eɪ – ə]	[æ – ə]
[ə]	[æ – ɔː]	[æ – ə]	[ə]	[ɑː – ə]
[eɪ]	[ə – eɪ – ə]	[æ – eɪ – ə]	[eɪ – ə]	[ɒ – eɪ – ə]

C.

Jánu(a)ry	Márch	Máy	Julý	Septémber	Novémber
Féb(r)u(a)ry	Ápr(i)l	Júne	Aúgust	Octóber	Decémber

D. (a) I thought you were one of the ones who won an award at the bazaar on Thursday.
(b) I bought you some more oranges and a pound of bananas at the greengrocer's that's just opened at the corner of Earl's Court Gardens.
(c) You can see from her early work that there's a certain sense of purpose, almost of urgency, which she appears to have lost as soon as she started to be accepted as a serious artist.
(d) More than a thousand representatives from the whole of the Third World were present at the concert given in the park yesterday afternoon to commemorate the anniversary of the birth of Ernest Hurlingham.
(e) There was an extraordinary man at your party who said that for years and years he'd been wanting to meet us. He said he would have asked the Templetons to introduce us, but he hadn't seen them for ages and didn't know what had happened to them.